The Tao of Running

For Cassie, Barney, Hobbs, Jubilee, Bonkers, Sebastian, Hermes, and
Patches:
They showed me the Way.

And many thanks to those who have shared the many miles of trails
with me: David Nakashima, Jeff Harber, Richard Schwarz, Karen
Cruz, Kathleen Bortolussi, Robert Josephs, and especially my excellent
friend, Rob Mann

GARY DUDNEY

THE TAO OF
RUNNING

YOUR JOURNEY TO MINDFUL AND
PASSIONATE RUNNING

Meyer & Meyer Sport

British Library Cataloguing in Publication Data
A catalogue record for this book is available from the British Library

The Tao of Running
Maidenhead: Meyer & Meyer Sport (UK) Ltd., 2016
ISBN: 978-1-78255-075-4

© 2016 by Meyer & Meyer Sport (UK) Ltd.
Aachen, Auckland, Beirut, Cairo, Cape Town, Dubai, Hägendorf, Hong Kong,
Indianapolis, Manila, New Delhi, Singapore, Sydney, Tehran, Vienna
Member of the World Sport Publishers' Association (WSPA)
Printed & Binded: CPI – Clausen & Bosse, Leck, Germany
E-Mail: info@m-m-sports.com
www.m-m-sports.com

TABLE OF CONTENTS

© Rob Mann

The author temporarily overwhelmed with the joy of running while crossing the famous No Hands Bridge at the Western States 100 Mile Endurance Run.

PROLOGUE

JUMPING OFF

"A good traveler has no fixed plans and is not intent on arriving."

From Lao Tzu, *Tao Te Ching*

Imagine for a moment that you take a chair from your dining room and position it in the center of your living room. Now take off your shoes and step up on the chair. Watch your balance. Now jump off the chair onto the carpet, or, if you're landing on a hardwood floor, bend your knees a little more to cushion the blow.

That wasn't such a big deal, was it? It didn't require you to think about it much. You didn't get emotionally invested in it. It wasn't much of a commitment. It didn't involve summoning much passion on your part. It certainly didn't change your life, although if anybody was watching, they might have been looking at you a little funny.

Now imagine a second jump except this time you're going to jump from a platform on a bridge that spans a deep river gorge. It's going to be a bungee jump. You stand there waiting in a fever pitch. You feel the wind on your face. You feel your heart beating in your chest. Light pours down from a glaring sun. The gorge under you is monstrous. All your senses are ultra sharp. You can pick out streaks of white water on the surface of the blue river rushing far below as if you were inspecting it through a telescope. The cars that roar by on the bridge behind you sound like raging locomotives. You smell the exhaust from their engines.

Now you feel the harness being tightened around you, the carabineers snapping into place. The whole world narrows down to a single focal point: your intense and monolithic commitment to jump. It is like nothing else has ever happened in your life, and nothing else ever will. Everything is all right now. You summon all your passion, hear the final countdown, feel vast emotions wash over you, and then you step off the platform completely and utterly in the moment. You exit the life you had before the bungee jump and enter your new life, the one after the bungee jump.

Now here is the point. The running experiences you are having right now are like jumping off the chair in your living room. The running experiences you are going to have after you read this book will be like the bungee jump. You are going to learn how to *think* about running and how to appreciate all of the rich possibilities inherent in running.

And it doesn't matter what kind of runner you are—a casual jogger, a solid 10K performer, a trail runner, a mud runner, a multi-time marathon finisher, a Spartan runner, an ultrarunner—everyone's running experience will be transformed and enhanced. You'll learn to bring passion, emotion, and total commitment to your running. You'll learn to be fully present in the moment, to live fully in the world, to run with the Tao.

Running is more than the sum of its parts. The physical side of it is pretty straightforward, but the psychological, the emotional, the philosophical dimensions of running are not as obvious. This book will deepen your understanding of those aspects of running, show you how running connects with the broader passions and aspirations in your life, and teach you how running can help you cope with life's challenges. You'll be motivated to run, eager to run, and ready to use running to transform your life.

In these pages, you'll explore how running connects with mindfulness, positivity, relaxation, the philosophy of existentialism, the concept of the Tao, the naturalistic elements of Buddhism, and other areas of life such as friendships. Each new perspective will open your eyes to the rich possibilities for self-growth and self-awareness that can be found in running. You'll learn new ways to think about goals and what is really important in the process of setting and achieving goals. You'll learn how to cope with the special demands of racing. You'll see how the friendships you make while running are unique. You'll discover the special benefits of trail running and learn how to become a "trail monster." You'll see how running works for many as a veritable fountain of health and youth.

If running has gotten boring for you or just feels like more work, this book will help you step back and see running in a whole new light. If you've ever flagged during a workout, lost your will, broken down in a marathon, or even dropped out of a race, this book will give you so many ways to stick with the program when the going gets tough that your problem will be deciding which one to use.

So never mind the dining room chair. Get yourself out of the living room and out the door. Get into the sunlight, feel the wind on your face, summon your passion. Then don't just step off that platform, leap off of it into the clear air.

WHY THE *TAO* OF RUNNING?

There is a traditional subject matter in Chinese painting of the three vinegar tasters. One interpretation of this subject matter holds that the three tasters represent the three great Chinese religions: Confucianism, Buddhism, and Taoism. The Confucian taster reacts to the vinegar with a sour expression, supposedly signifying how his philosophy finds life sour since the present is thought to be out of step with the past. The Buddhist reacts with a bitter expression because life, according to his philosophy, is bitter in that it is full of pain and suffering. But the Taoist tastes the vinegar and takes on a sweet expression. Sweet?

For the Taoist, the taste of the vinegar is not the issue. The Taoist recognizes that the vinegar is simply being vinegar; it is being true to its nature in the natural order of things, which for a Taoist is intrinsically good. By experiencing the vinegar as it is, non-judgmentally, the Taoist himself is recognizing and participating in the flowing and harmonious universe that Taoism posits.

A key goal of Taoism is to fit into this harmonious flow in our approach to all things and in all our actions. A Taoist has a particular way of appreciating and learning from and working with whatever happens in life. Any situation one finds oneself in, like tasting the vinegar, might be unpleasant or it might involve conflict or some disconcerting change, but the Taoist brings an attitude of acceptance to life and recognizes that whatever the situation, this is life just being life and things change and evolve.

Now, instead of three vinegar tasters, let's think of two runners. They take the same path through a park and run the same distance, but how they experience the run, their perception of the run, and their attitudes toward the run may vary widely. One runner, like the Confucian taster or the Buddhist taster, may find the run stressful or uncomfortable— that is, sour or bitter and finish the run with no appreciation for it. The other runner may take a Taoist approach, accept the run as it is, see it clearly, learn from it, perhaps discover a new essence in it previously unknown or unappreciated, and sink down into the experience of the run. In this book, we will take the Taoist approach. We will explore ways to see running clearly, to discover the essence of running, and to sink down into the experience of running. We will search for the Tao of running.

© Gary Dudney

Why are we so eager to run? Why do we enjoy running so much?

CHAPTER 1

WHAT IS IT ABOUT RUNNING?

What is it about running, anyway? We go out for a little jog, a little exercise, and the habit grows. Each day we go a little farther. Our sights lengthen. One mile begins to feel paltry, and we extend ourselves. Before long, we are training, preparing for a race. The training gets more focused. The number of minutes it takes to run each mile shrinks as our speed and power grow. The habit has caught on. We circle a track, chasing seconds now, cleaving the quarter-mile time or the half-mile time as precisely as a diamond.

We pile up the intervals and the training sessions and then find ourselves in a 5K or a 10K, straining to hold our pace. The middle miles of the 10K become a test of character, the final mile a test of will, grit, and courage. Our sights lengthen again, and we take on longer distances. Each week we pile up the miles; each weekend we extend our long runs. Eventually we line up in the big cities with thousands of others, with the goal far away—26 miles away. A gun goes off, and we launch into a rite of passage, a bucket list quest, a journey that will take us far along the road and deep within ourselves.

The agony near the marathon's end is like fire, burning fiercely but cleansing. At the final moment, we burst out of the flames, cross the finish line, and are reborn into our lives, returned from a deep inner journey. But having returned, we are not the same.

Really, we had only thought to go for a little jog, but one thing led to another, one run led to another, and now running has insinuated itself into our very being, and we are runners, as, it seems upon reflection, we were meant to be.

THE RUNNING BOOM

In the United States, mass participation in running exploded onto the scene in the early 70s, inspired by American Frank Shorter's victory in the marathon at the 1972 Munich Olympics. And what remarkable Olympic Games those were! It was Germany's first stint as host of the Summer Games since the infamous Games in Berlin of 1936. By 1972, television coverage had improved and expanded, so people could indulge their passion for the Games. People in the United States had always loved the Olympic ideals of peaceful competition, pursuit of excellence, and supreme victory of the individual athlete over competitors from around the world. And here were the Games right in our living rooms.

But in the second week of the Games, Palestinian terrorists upended everything using the enormous stage of the Olympics to proclaim their grievances and murder Israeli athletes. A photo of one of the masked terrorists on the balcony in the Olympic Village fixed the horror in everyone's minds for all time. Then came the courageous decision by the Olympic Committee, the German officials, the Israeli government, and the athletes to continue the competitions, and thus the stage for running the marathon was set.

Americans were watching by way of a live satellite feed from Munich as the runners circled the track in the stadium, which really looked at first like a common track and field ho-hum affair, but then suddenly all the runners followed a line of barricades off the track into a large tunnel that whisked them right out of the stadium and onto the streets of Munich. We were used to seeing Olympic competitions staged inside stadiums or in field houses, in giant swimming halls or in gymnasiums. It was stunning to see the marathon runners out on the streets and sidewalks, people walking, cars driving by, life going on as if a major Olympic event weren't happening right under their noses.

Shorter hung back from the leaders in the first stages of the race in about tenth place. Nobody expected anything special of him that day, but at mile nine, he made a bold move, a breakaway right off the front, opening up a significant lead. When no one came to chase him down, he remembers saying to himself, "They're making a big mistake."

Shorter never faltered. In a white racing singlet, blue shorts, wearing number 1014 just below the "USA" emblazoned on his singlet, the mustachioed Shorter ran solo the rest of the way. The runners behind him were tying up, bending sideways trying to relieve awful cramps, collapsing to the ground, but Shorter ran along unfazed. He maintained a strong, upright, almost relaxed-looking stride. His face was impassive.

At home, Americans could hardly believe what they were seeing. This was the marathon, the province of only true fanatics and Olympic gods, a distance really quite unimaginable for most of the viewers, who would have considered five miles an extremely long run. Here was an American winning, looking relaxed, and making mincemeat out of the competition. How incomparably, unutterably cool was that?

At the end of the race, some joker in a track outfit snuck through the barriers and cruised around the track in the stadium just as Shorter arrived. The crowd was jeering, realizing the hoax, which made Shorter wonder what was going on. Jim McKay and the other American announcers were beside themselves. McKay claimed Shorter was confused. "He doesn't know what to do," he said. The other announcer, Erich Segal, spoke as if directly to Shorter, "Frank, you won it…Frank, it's a fake, Frank." But Shorter said later he never even saw the other runner. He was not confused about winning, just about why the crowd seemed to be jeering instead of cheering.

Meanwhile, back home in the United States, people were fired up. The seeds of the running boom had been flung far and wide across the land. Running was suddenly a very "in" thing to do at a time when being "in" was really very "in."

People took to the streets in droves. You didn't need a track team. You didn't need smelly liniment oil. You didn't have to do laps on a track. You could just go outside and run on the roads. The fusty old running federations and local committees that held running competitions and focused mainly on the most competitive runners gave way to organizations that were more inclusive. Running clubs formed. Races sprang up everywhere. Women were allowed into the Boston Marathon. Shoe and apparel companies got on board. Frank Shorter became one hero among many, including Bill Rodgers, Alberto Salazar, Steve Prefontaine, Jim Ryun, Mary Decker, and Grete Waitz. In 1984, in Los

Angeles, Joan Benoit matched Shorter's feat with a going-away win at the first ever Olympic Marathon held for women.

The incredible interest and thirst for information about running became apparent in 1977 with the publication of Jim Fixx's, *The Complete Book of Running*. At the time, it was the leading best-selling non-fiction hardcover book on the market. The jacket cover of the book, a striking deep-red, featured a close-up of Fixx's own legs with every muscle, tendon, and sinew sharply defined. The legs sprouted out of red running shorts and were punctuated with classic red and white-striped Onitsuka Tiger racing flats.

Fixx jumped into his topic on page 1. He was not out to help you drop a few pounds or introduce you to a neat fitness technique. No, Jim Fixx was going to change your life, and dramatically, if you would only run on a regular basis. Fixx proselytized for running. He saw running as a magic elixir, a fountain of youth, a key to physical and mental health. This message was pretty much news to people back in 1977. Of course, running had always been considered good exercise. It was something US Marines supposedly did for five miles every day. But people didn't imagine it was going to change their lives. What exactly was Fixx smoking?

From today, looking back some forty years to when running became widespread, we can see that Fixx wasn't smoking anything. On the contrary, he was on to something. Running has persisted. The running boom had legs!

Running or jogging became the go-to exercise routine for millions, and the increase in the number of structured running events has reflected the growing demand. In addition to the proliferation of shorter distance races, we've seen the establishment of a vast circuit of marathons,

WHAT IS IT ABOUT RUNNING?

most of them big city affairs that draw participation in the tens of thousands and constitute a whole lifestyle subculture for many. Clubs form just to facilitate their membership, entering marquee marathons all over the world. In addition to the popularity of the marathon, you have millions stepping off road to sample trail running with the result that trail races have become commonplace, and there is no shortage of runners who are stepping up to the more extreme distances of ultrarunning. Even one hundred-mile races are getting so many entrants that lotteries must be held to determine the starting field. In short, not only has the running boom not faded with time, but it has grown and spawned new formats to meet an insatiable demand for the sport.

Generally speaking, other sports can't make similar claims about their lasting popularity. At the same 1972 Summer Games where Shorter prevailed in the marathon, American swimmer Mark Spitz totally dominated in the pool, winning seven gold medals over an impressive mix of events. But where was a lasting wide spread swimming boom? Greg Limond won cycling's Tour de France three times, an unparalleled feat for an American, but though interest in road cycling went up, there was no lasting cycling boom. Nadia Comaneci and her perfect ten at the Olympic Games in Montreal in 1976 inspired enormous interest and participation in gymnastics, but the movement only went so far. The same can be said of soccer in America, mountain biking, skiing, hiking, golf, and surfing. Interest in these activities grows and wans. Lots of people enjoy these sports and get a lot out of them, but all pale in comparison to what has happened with running.

So what is it about running anyway? Why does running appeal to so many people? Why does running invoke so much passion and commitment? Why has completing a marathon, for example, become such a singular goal, a bucket list goal, for so many?

RUNNING IS IN OUR GENES

In evolutionary terms, running, in many important respects, is who we are. Our bodies exhibit many adaptations that not only allow us to function as bipedal, upright walkers, but also appear specifically suited for long-distance running. We have tendons, ligaments, and muscles that act like elastic springs, briefly storing and releasing energy, propelling us forward efficiently when we run. Our muscles are loaded with fatigue-resistant, slow-twitch muscle fibers. Increased joint surfaces spread out the shock and force applied to joints when impacting the ground. The plantar arches and the prominent Achilles tendons are specialized features that enhance running ability. Our large gluteus maximus muscles promote stability. All these adaptations are far beyond the requirements of just being able to walk upright. They combine with several other adaptations to make us long-distance champion runners in the animal kingdom.

Our *Australopithecus* precursors mostly lacked these specific features. At some point on the way to *Homo erectus*, running apparently became a critical survival factor, and, according to the endurance running hypothesis, the human body evolved rapidly to maximize its ability to outlast other animals when on the move. A critical component of this development was an increased capacity to dissipate heat and to store and utilize energy. Put us out in the heat, and sweating keeps us cool for long periods. The animals we're chasing, on the other hand, can only stay cool for a while by panting. Eventually they overheat. We also have an advantage in how our energy stores are utilized and the way we can vary our diet to meet prolonged energy demands. Put all these advantages together, and, the theory goes, we are uniquely evolved to run down our prey, especially in hot conditions.

No wonder, then, that when we run we experience a profound connection to our physical selves. Maybe at first what we perceive most are our joints creaking, our muscles tightening and aching, our respiration laboring, and our cooling system failing to do the job, but as we gain fitness and all these components of running adjust and improve, we begin to feel like the running animal that we became as the result of eons of natural selection. We run and we engage our bodies in just the way that our bodies were designed to be engaged. The movement of running is harmonious with the body we are moving, and the body that is being moved, well, that is you. And as the body is engaged, so, too, is the mind. The mind exists in association with the body, with the physical, so there is no surprise that your mind responds to this natural motion, this momentous coming together of you with your body's most fundamental essence.

THE RUNNING ESCAPE

For most of us, running represents a sharp contrast from what we are doing with the rest of our day. At work, we are tied to a desk, sitting, bombarded with emails, phone calls, demanding bosses, and stress. Or we are performing a repetitive, annoying task on a workshop floor, or we are wheedling information out of a customer, looking for an opening to make another sale. At home, we are overburdened with chores, family problems, money concerns, and the constant lure of mostly trashy entertainment. The chance to escape, at least for a little while, from our cares and concerns, to leave it all behind, and to go out for a run is a golden opportunity to connect back with ourselves and forget temporarily about life's tribulations.

We hit the locker room, or the bedroom, or wherever the liberating changing of the clothes will occur. The shirt and tie or the silk blouse comes off and on goes a slinky, breathable, technical t-shirt. Off comes the pleated skirt or the neatly creased slacks to be replaced by loose, lightweight running shorts. The legs are blessedly free now — free to stretch, free to move. On our feet, we trade leather for a pair of magical, modern, highly designed, protective running shoes, or fun little slippers if we have gone down the minimalist path. We apply the sunblock, don the hat, and are out the door.

The first few strides on the pavement or in the dirt feel like a release from bondage, a launch into space. We almost gasp at the transition from sedentary, constrained, physical inaction to the pure natural motion of running. Our minds lighten, and our spirits soar. Just the motion alone is cathartic and transformative.

Who can blame us if, in those first few steps out the door, we feel like we're flying?

THE RUNNING BODY

Once we're running, many things begin to happen. Just in terms of exercising, running is the bomb, especially when it comes to cardiorespiratory or cardiovascular fitness. Running promotes lower blood pressure, lower cholesterol, greater bone mass and stronger muscles, and revs up your metabolism. As a calorie burner, running is a blast furnace, topping most other forms of exercise, and the burn continues after you stop. Regular exercise contributes to what is called *excess post-exercise oxygen consumption,* that is, while you're sitting around after exercising watching TV, your body is still gobbling calories at an accelerated rate.

Running fights age-related bone loss. The old shibboleth that running is bad for your knees is not borne out by studies, which instead show that runners don't develop osteoarthritis any faster than non-runners, and runners, in fact, often show improved knee health. All the many health benefits derived from running, not surprisingly, contribute to longevity. And while you're living longer, you're staying mentally sharper as the regular exercise running provides has been shown to reduce age-related mental decline. Regular exercise has even been shown to lower the risk of contracting cancer. So what's not to like about running? You slim down, you live longer, you're healthier, and you can still do the tough crossword puzzles in the Sunday paper. Running also gives you a nice espresso shot of self-esteem.

THE RUNNING MIND

The physical benefits of running alone are worth the price of admission, but they are only part of the story. We run, and the mind is set free, or, more precisely, the mind begins to operate in the context of the body in full physical realization of its genetically engineered potential. The rhythm of the stride, the metronome of the swinging arms, the exertion, the working of all the key running muscles, and especially the concentrated, regular, deep breathing create conditions much like one experiences when one meditates. The mind moves away from the mundane concerns of everyday life and is free to engage in more creative or more fundamental thinking.

If nothing else, running is a break from the work world or the world of daily nagging concerns. Running time can be a worry-free zone. Once you're out the door, on the streets, or on the trail, there is no obligation to think about problems. You're fixing a problem. You're getting your exercise and making yourself healthier and stronger so that you can go back and face up to your concerns. But, paradoxically, running can promote a state of mind in which, if you do focus on a work problem or a relationship issue, you often discover creative solutions or at least new possibilities that would never have occurred to you sitting at your desk or folding laundry. When your mind is free to roam, it often finds its way to new places.

Running draws your mind away from its usual concerns and into the physical world, both because you are performing a physical exercise and because you are now surrounded by and immersed in the physical world—the sights, sounds, smells, and feel of the outdoors. Suddenly life is very immediate, very sensual, and very real. For the time we are running, we are in touch with the natural world and in touch with ourselves in a very direct way. Many runners find this extremely gratifying and will tell you that they run because they like to be in the mountains, in the forest, or out in nature. Wouldn't a good hike accomplish the same purpose? Apparently not. It's the running in conjunction with being in the mountains or in the forest that seems to bring on the magic. Trail running is a massive phenomenon right now with explosive growth in the numbers of participants and organized events. Do we see the same growth in hiking? Not so much.

It is small wonder, then, that running can lead us into a Taoist frame of mind. As we enter deeper into the rhythms of nature, as we let go of our egos and free ourselves from daily superficial thoughts, we seem to come into harmony with the world around us. Taoists liken becoming one with Tao to water being poured into water. Running can be seen in a similar light. In the physical act of running, we pour ourselves into the physical world. The running takes on a flow and seems effortless, natural, and profoundly satisfying. There is a lack of restraint in the way we move, and there is an openness to the beauty of things around us.

But there are other ways to think about running, other ways to interpret the deeper inner pathways that we explore when we pursue running consistently and passionately. Running can be an excellent vehicle for practicing mindfulness, for quieting our overburdened minds, and for focusing with full attention on the present moment. Running can also be a very existential activity, leading us to feel directly alive in the moment in a way that we seldom experience in any other aspects of our lives. As we run, we tend to drop all our social roles—our pretenses, our masks, our self-defense mechanisms that crowd into our daily existence. Out on the trail, these things are essentially irrelevant. While we are running, we tend to just exist very intensely. We are, as existentialists say, simply "being in the world."

In whatever philosophical light we may bring to examine running, the universal experience seems to be transcendence. In running, we transcend our usual selves, our workaday egos, and we are freed to explore things that are perhaps more profound.

Runners explore not only a vast outer landscape, but a vast inner landscape of the mind as well.

© Gary Dudney

RUNNING WITH PASSION

In conjunction with this deep dive into our minds that running promotes, running evokes in many a very deeply seated passion. Just look at the marathon craze and the way completing a marathon has become a singular, overarching goal for so many. The world's greatest marathons now draw crowds of thousands and thousands, but what is special is that the crowds are not there to watch and experience the sport vicariously; the crowds are there to run the race, to participate, to actually be in the arena. And having done the training, endured the race, and tasted the supreme satisfaction of the finish, many runners come back over and over again.

And, of course, there are the ultrarunners for whom even the 26-mile distance is somehow not enough. They complete a 31-mile 50K race, graduate to the 50-mile race, go on to the 62-mile 100K race, and then, as if they were just getting warmed up, they take on the mythic challenge of running 100 miles in a single day. And when they are done, dirt covering their legs, bleary eyed, limping and listing to avoid antagonizing the blisters covering their feet, they look up and with wonder in their voices tell you that it was like living a whole lifetime out there.

Running is replete with goals—setting goals, striving for goals, reaching one's potential, finding one's limits, gaining self-knowledge, being passionate about the goal, and by extension being passionate about one's own life. We can pursue running a particular distance. We can pursue running a particular time. We train toward a whole set of intermediate goals. There are daily goals, weekly goals, monthly goals, and lifetime goals. The goals in running are wonderfully concrete. You want to break 40 minutes in the 10K. You will either do that, or you won't. There is not going to be any ambiguity about it. You want to finish a marathon. You either cross the finish line, or you don't. Case closed.

But, oddly, in the end, reaching the goal is not really the point. You may accomplish your goal because you had the genetic potential to run a three-hour marathon, and you trained really hard, and you cultivated the mental attitude that allowed you to endure such a hard, fast pace, and you made it. But then maybe you didn't make it. Maybe as hard as you tried, you just didn't have the potential to run that far, that fast. Maybe the training wasn't all there. Maybe the strain broke you psychologically when you hit the wall. It doesn't matter. It's not really reaching the goal that matters. What matters is the journey.

The journey of running is the issue here. That is what I want you to understand more fully: the amazing, passionate, mysterious journey of running and how running can promote self-awareness and self-improvement. In the pages that follow, you will find many ways to think about running, many perspectives from which you can examine your running experiences, many frameworks that you can use to better understand and appreciate what is happening to you as you run. Being aware of these connections between running and mindfulness, running and Taoism, and running and the pursuit of goals will help you get more out of your running and almost certainly more out of your life.

WHAT IS IT ABOUT RUNNING?

CHAPTER 2

TRIPPING

It was the middle of the night, two o'clock, to be exact, on a Sunday in early March. I was hurrying along a narrow, rocky trail high up on the side of Nordoff Ridge above Ojai, California, in a cold, hard rain. I struggled to see through my fogged glasses. Spots of light from my headlamp and flashlight bounced all over the trail. And then, with no warning, I was going down.

I'd caught a rock squarely with my toe and felt a sick, sudden, uncontrolled lurch into space. My newly patched-up left collarbone led the way downward. I imagined the impact, the titanium bar holding the ends of my bone together twisting into a paperclip and the six screws exploding out of the bone and ripping through my flesh.

I had shattered my clavicle a couple of months before riding a mountain bike, which I was doing instead of running because I was recovering from foot surgery. Shoot, all I'd done was slightly mistime lifting my front tire over an asphalt curb that separated the road from the trail. An eye blink later, I was sitting in the dust thinking how ironic it was that I'd just broken my left collarbone so close to where I'd broken my right collarbone on the very same trail a year before in another mountain biking mishap. That time I was wearing a fancy biker's shirt that showed a skeleton with its right clavicle in two pieces, which occasioned quite a big laugh from the hospital staff in the emergency room.

My doctor had me follow the now familiar treatment of just letting the fracture heal naturally. After allowing time for this to happen, weeks of physical therapy ensued with the therapist leveraging all her weight on my arm saying, "Gee, you're so weak." Turns out the ends of the bone hadn't knit together, so I had been trying to fight her off with a bone in two separate pieces. The next doctor I saw recommended surgery. "Shall we really fix it this time?" he asked. Now I was post-surgery, and with a little recovery time and a cold chunk of titanium humming just beneath my skin, I was back and ready to take on the Coyote Two Moon 100-Mile Trail Run, a monster endurance run that relentlessly climbs and descends a 5,000-foot ridge above the Ojai and Rose Valleys in southern California.

We started the race at nine o'clock on Friday night, laboring up a steep rocky trail into a light rain that soon turned heavy. Then came the fog, so thick that I had to take off my headlamp and hold it down by my knees to keep the light from reflecting back and blinding me. As the night wore on, we reached the top of Topa Ridge where the rain had become a blowing snowstorm. And so it went. We'd drop down off the ridge out of snow into icy rain and then climb back into snow and then repeat all Saturday morning and afternoon and into the second night.

By the time I was sitting at the aid station at Gridley Bottom late Saturday night with just one major climb left between me and a prized finisher's belt buckle, I was pretty spent. The incessant cold rain wasn't letting up. I was trying to make sense out of the jumble of clothes, batteries, electrolyte pills, and energy gels spilling out of my drop bag at my feet in the mud. The ham radio operator was announcing that the race director, who was at an aid station on top of the ridge, was saying no one without at least long pants to protect them from the cold was allowed to come back up. The guy next to me was getting a towel fastened around his waist like a long skirt so he could continue. In order to not freeze to death sitting there, I pushed out of my chair, waited for a second to let the lightheadedness pass, and then started trudging back up the trail.

I climbed past a bizarre avocado orchard, up a steep jeep road, and then made my way along a single track that had become a fast flowing stream. I passed the place where earlier that night coming down I had convinced myself I was on the wrong trail. At the time, my exhausted brain was telling me the trail should drop straight down to the aid station, so when I took a sharp turn into a yawning black canyon, it didn't look right. It had been hours since I'd seen anyone else on the trail. Where were the people who should be coming back up? I shined my light into the distance, but the puny beam was no match for the vast black void ahead of me. I reasoned that if anyone were anywhere in those miles below me, I would surely see some kind of light bouncing around down there. I stopped and yelled into the pouring rain, "Hello... hello!" My pathetic, thin voice died around me like a lifeless jellyfish.

© Gary Dudney

Into the fog and cold...

Certain now I must be lost, I headed back up the trail to look for the turn I thought I'd missed, cursing at having to add distance to my run. A seeming eternity later, I spotted two lights coming toward me. A couple of runners appeared splashing down the trail, both soaked to the gills just like me. "Are you guys sure this is the right trail?" I asked.

The first runner went by looking annoyed. "What other trail is there?" he said and kept going.

"I went down a long ways, and there's nobody there," I said to their backs. They slowed down, stopped and turned to look at me. The one who had spoken before put his hands on his hips, ducked his head, thinking.

Finally he said, "Ain't no other trail," and off they went.

I hesitated, but I had to admit that they looked like they had their shit together. I was pretty sure that I did not, so I followed them. The trail seemed to go impossibly far down into the canyon, but eventually it proved to be correct and got us to Gridley Bottom.

Now I was on my way back up, pushing for the top, for the last aid station before I could cross along the ridge and drop down to the finish line. But the higher I got, the harder the wind seemed to be blowing. A constant howl swept down on me from above. The rain around me had turned to driving snow. I figured I must be getting close to the final section of trail that angled up to the aid station on the ridge when I saw lights from a group of runners cutting through the snow coming toward me. Three runners appeared, a woman bracketed by two men.

© Gary Dudney

A little sampling of the rocky trail on Nordhoff Ridge above Ojai.

The woman, blonde hair sticking out from underneath a black knit cap, wearing a red jacket and black tights, said, "It's canceled. Everyone is supposed to get down off the ridge."

"What?" I heard myself shout.

"There's a total blizzard on the ridge. People don't have the right clothes. The race director decided it was too dangerous, so he's sending everybody down. It's over. No race."

"Are you absolutely certain?" I pleaded. I couldn't believe it. Hundred-mile races weren't supposed to be easy. You were supposed to have to deal with bad stuff. Sure I was cold, but they had a heater going in the tent at the aid station up above. I'd seen it. I was planning a long rest there. I'd get dried out, and then nothing could stop me from covering those last six or seven miles on the ridge and then heading down to the finish to claim my buckle.

"We gotta get going," one of the guys said. "I'm freezing."

"It's canceled," the woman said as she turned and ran after her buddies.

I stood there. Then I took a few more steps toward the top. Then I stopped. How close was I to the aid station? Should I go on up and see for myself? But I realized, even if I got up there and saw the race director and convinced him I could make it, I wasn't going to get an official finish. If the race was done, then no one was getting anything. I could hear the wind whistling over the ridge. I faced the facts. There was nothing left to do but go back down.

The group that had given me the bad news had disappeared into the darkness. I began to rush downward to catch them, splashing through the water on the trail, careening over the baseball-sized rocks scattered everywhere, cornering through the mud down twisting switchbacks. That's when I caught my foot on a half-buried rock that wasn't moving.

For a moment I was stretched out in the air, and then everything hit at once. My thigh, my hip, my torso, my shoulder, the side of my head— everything slammed into the trail together, which actually was a good thing. It distributed the force and the pain democratically all over my body. I slid down through the cold mud, feeling it lathering up against the side of my face. Instantly, I popped back up, as if getting back on my feet could somehow take back what had just happened. I sucked for the air that had been knocked out of me and stood there dazed. My hat and headlamp were in the mud at my feet. My flashlight dangled from my wrist from its lanyard, the light bouncing crazily around my feet. There was a solid thick layer of mud stuck to my side that ran from my hair all the way down to my shoes.

I reached up and felt that my shoulder was still there and seemed intact. No titanium bar sticking out of my skin or stray screws. Both my arms worked. There were no open wounds along my side. I'd lucked out and missed the rocks. I wiped the mud off my jacket as best I could and wiped a handful off my face. I fished my hat and headlamp out of the mud, put on the hat, and felt a cold stream of water dribble down my back. I cleaned the flashlight off on the unmuddy side of my running pants, and then set off at a slow trot. *Careful*, I told myself. *Relax. One step at a time. Every step gets you closer to being down.*

Surprisingly, even moving slowly, it didn't take long to catch up with the three runners who had left me behind. And they had caught some other runners, so there was a train of eight or nine of us heading down the trail. I fell in behind. No one spoke. Everyone was too cold, miserable, discouraged, disappointed, and beaten up to talk. The pace was slow, slower than I had been going. I told myself to just follow the guy ahead of me, place my feet where he had, and be patient, but now that I wasn't working so hard, I started getting a chill. Before long my teeth were chattering, and that nice warm feeling in my chest telling me that my core temperature was okay even if my extremities were getting cold was fading into an icy chill.

I tried to hold out. I told myself to just stay with the program, but the teeth chattering was getting worse and now I was shivering off and on, sometimes really shaking hard. I had to do something. "Can I get by, please?" I asked. The guy in front of me stepped aside. I worked my way down through the whole group, and when the last runner moved over, I took off. I had to run harder to generate more heat. I had to get down where it was slightly warmer. I made it to the jeep road and pointed my light well ahead of me so I could speed up. I noticed another light at my feet and realized someone was following me.

"I had to go faster," I yelled over my shoulder. "I was freezing to death."

"Same here," the other runner said.

So we worked it together down off the jeep road and onto the final awful single track, a frightful trail that was full of boulder-sized rocks that were a challenge to scramble over even in broad daylight. In the rain, in the dark, it was a nightmare. At last I saw the lights of the aid station below and heard the growling roar of a big generator. The heavy rain had people dashing from the aid station tent to cars and back. A few runners were huddled around a bonfire, holding jackets over their heads. I spotted a van on the edge of the clearing with its engine going and two runners already inside. I went straight for it and opened the side door. "Are you going back to the start/finish?" I asked.

The driver reached back and threw a towel over the open seat in front of me. "Get in," he said.

I jumped in and shut the door. I could feel the warm air from the van's heater on my face, but my whole body was still covered in frigid wet clothing. I sat and shivered, clutching my hydration pack to my chest, my elbows glued to my sides, my hands shaking. Someone came and took my race number. I was officially down from the ridge now. I could be checked off. Other runners crowded into the van. Every time the door opened, cold air flooded in and thoroughly refrigerated me.

The drive back to the start/finish was a confusion of windshield wipers, pounding rain, flashing lights, and splashing tires. We reached the road that led up to the field where the race had begun. Our cars were scattered up and down the road, stuck in breaks between the trees and brush that bordered the asphalt. I searched for my car in the black, wet confusion outside the window. The van's lights caught tree branches, a set of cars, more branches, shrubs, more cars.

"There!" I said, when I saw my car, a silver SUV at the top of a group of four or five cars in one of the tree breaks. The van stopped, and I climbed out as well as my stiff limbs would allow and thanked the driver. Off went the van, and I turned into the rain and ran to my car. The water was coming down so hard now it almost seemed like some cosmic joke—the heaviest, coldest rain possible at the worst possible time. The slight gain I'd made on getting warm in the van vanished. I was freezing cold again, the icy rain splashing off my already soaked clothes. I fumbled with the key. I could barely get my fingers to work. I hit the unlock button, but nothing happened. I jammed the key in the door and tried to twist. Nothing. My mind hit the panic button. *I must be doing something wrong*, I thought. *Slow down. Try again.* Nothing.

Then it struck me. I ran back into the road and looked farther up the street. Blackness. I ran forward a bit. There! Another break in the trees and sure enough, another four or five cars parked in a row with a silver SUV at the top. I felt a cry of frustration spontaneously burst out of me. I ran up to the SUV and hit the unlock button. This time lights flashed, and there was a click, click sound. I jumped inside, but I was so thoroughly cold my teeth were chattering again, and I was being racked with spasms, shivering violently. I started the car and twisted the heat and fan knobs full blast, but that only served to blow cold air all over me. I gripped the steering wheel to try and control the spasms. I felt like I was going to shake into pieces.

Then the blessed warmth started coming, little by little at first, and then, very suddenly, the air went from slightly warm to a full flood of hot comfort. I groaned with relief and felt the shivering dying down inside me and then finally ceasing. I was conscience of breathing again, as if I'd been holding my breath since I'd stepped out of the van. Soon enough, though, I became aware of just how soaking wet I was and realized there was a limit to how comfortable I was going to get even in a warm car.

I pulled a bag full of dry clothes off the backseat into the passenger's seat and zipped it open. As I leaned down to untie my shoe, I felt a ridiculously strong cramp on the side of my hip. I bolted upright to relieve the cramp and felt a calf muscle now knotting up. Flexing my foot upward helped that, but as soon as I leaned down to try my shoelace again, both hips cramped, and I had to straighten out again as best I could with the steering wheel in my way. I paused to catch my breath and let everything go neutral for a moment. I realized I'd stopped taking electrolyte tablets way up on the side of the ridge, and now my muscles were reacting to the depletion. I fished a couple of tablets out of my hydration pack.

This was the state of my shoes after the race was called off and everyone was down off the ridge.

41

I managed to get my shoes and wet socks off. The warm air blowing out of the lower vents felt like heaven on my bare skin. I arched up and got out of my wet tights and running shorts. I pulled on dry underwear and warm-up pants and then got into a dry sweatshirt. All the while I fought off cramps in my hips, calves, hamstrings, and a couple in my upper back. When I pointed my toes to put on dry socks, my foot went into a vicious cramp. I had to grab my toes and pull them back to relieve it. By the time I had both socks on, I was exhausted.

I looked at the clock in the dash—4:45 am. I had about seven hours before I could check into my hotel room. I thought of my wife home in bed and my kids at college, one in Los Angeles the other in New York. I'd told them I'd call when I got to the hotel. They'd assume everything was fine; I was finishing another crazy 100-mile race. Nothing special was going on. They wouldn't know the race had been cancelled when I was almost 90 miles into it, that there'd be no belt buckle, no finish.

They'd just expect to see me walk in the door with my buckle and a smile and some story about how hard it had been, but they'd just tune it out. There had been so many stories, and if you weren't doing it yourself, it just didn't seem all that real.

I looked out the window. The rain was a very steady, unbroken downpour, a continuous roar drumming on the top of the car, sheets of water streaming down the windows. Way up the road, there was a single streetlight shining in the dark. The light fractured crazily in the water on the windshield. Well beyond the streetlamp was a turn off from the road into the field where the start/finish was, where I had begun running at nine o'clock Friday night. Now the sun was about to come up Sunday morning.

It had been a long struggle. I was all alone, and home was far away. I was incredibly tired. I put the seat back and closed my eyes, letting the warm air play over me. At least I was dry, and if I kept very still, it kept the cramps at bay.

A question popped into my mind, something I had really not thought much about before: Why exactly was I doing this? Why was I out here all alone, in the worst weather imaginable, in the middle of the night, trying to run 100 miles of godforsaken rough trail for a belt buckle? Why had running become such a big part of my life? It was something I realized I needed to think about, something I needed to understand.

CHAPTER 3

DECONSTRUCTING ROCKY BALBOA

It's 1979. The running boom is in full swing, and no holiday or festival is complete without its accompanying 5K or 10K race. Wichita, Kansas, is celebrating the anniversary of its founding in 1870 with a newly minted river festival, and true to form, there is an associated Wichita River Run 10K. It's my first ever organized race, and I have no earthly idea what I'm doing, but I do know that I'm in running hell.

My legs are solid blocks of granite, almost impossible to lift and move forward. My lungs are bursting like I'm trying to suck air through a six-foot-long straw. My face is so contorted with agony, I imagine children running away at the sight of me screaming, "Mommy, Mommy! What are they doing to that man?" My vision has narrowed and blurred. I'm running through a bucolic riverside park, but to me it all looks like a cave of horrors. My panicky brain is screaming, "Where, oh God, is the finish line?"

Suddenly someone moves up on my elbow. It is a young girl. She looks to be about half my age, maybe 13 or 14. Her face is all pink from the exertion of running. Pigtails trail out from under her cap. She has round, soft-looking arms and legs, also pink. What is going on? How is this little girl matching me stride for stride and about to pass me? Oh, yes. I'm in running hell. It figures. A spectator in a fancy track suit comes bounding off the sidelines and pulls up next to the pink girl opposite me. He leans in and says, "C'mon, Bobbie, you can take this guy. Dig in, dig in. You can beat him." I rise above my agony and crane my head around to get a better look. The guy is snarling at her. He sounds angry. "Pass this guy, Bobbie. He's weak. He's faltering. You can do it. Lift your knees. Get him!"

Does the guy think I can't hear him? He just called me weak and faltering. Okay, granted, I am weak and faltering, but that's my business. My macho side gets all tweaked up into a massive hissy fit. There is no way now that I am going to let Bobbie beat me to the finish line.

I convulse like Uma Thurman in *Pulp Fiction* getting the hypodermic needle of adrenaline shot straight to her heart. The shackles fall away from my legs. My arms pump furiously. I gasp in chunks of fresh air. I am aware of my body lurching forward, but I no longer seem connected to it or in control of it. Through the roar in my mind, I can just make out Bobbie's coach berating her for letting me get away.

I storm across the finish line like I'm Roger Bannister breaking the four-minute mile, my head twisting, my arms thrown in the air. A little knot of people are clapping. I turn to see Bobbie finish. She looks despondent. I feel bad about beating her now. The guy in the track suit is coming up behind her, and he looks pissed off. I move away so I don't have to hear what he's going to say.

Back in those days, I think I was like a lot of runners at the time. I focused on training and on racing. When I ran, I didn't "go out for a jog." I "did a workout." I timed myself. I went to a track and did intervals. I took what could have been a pleasant, relaxed run through a wooded park on a cool breezy day and made it a tempo run, pushing myself the whole way, cursing myself if I slowed down, straining right up to the limit of my capabilities. Running was hard work. Getting faster was the goal.

When I first started running 10Ks, I could see a lot of progress from one race to the next, which was very heartening. But eventually I moved into a world of diminishing returns. I could run twice as far each week, do more tempo runs and more intervals, but my 10K results hardly budged. Instead of knocking whole minutes off my previous times, I would have to run the race of my life to lower my time by just a few seconds. No pain, no gain I could accept, but this was massive pain bordering on torture for practically zip gain. Who needed it? Running was like a bad job—lots of hassle and low rewards. Running sucked.

© Gary Dudney

A race lasts for only a few hours. Training for the race can go on for months, so it makes sense to enjoy the journey that you're on while you're training.

THE MARATHON BUG

Then I caught the marathon bug. Here was a new enthralling challenge to replace the stale, frustrating challenge that the 10K distance had become. I bumped up my mileage. I religiously lengthened my long runs from one weekend to the next. I built up to 20-mile runs. I even did a 22 miler and a 24 miler before my actual first marathon attempt. And being true to the zeitgeist of running in those days, I didn't just pad through those long runs, I hammered them. I ran down highways, checking my watch, keeping up my pace, measuring out those miles, and pushing harder when I felt like slowing down.

And never, ever, under any circumstances, cross my heart and hope to die, did I ever take a break and walk. Walking was for losers. If I was going to run a marathon, I was going to run the whole thing. Weren't you disqualified or something if they caught you walking?

Finishing that first marathon, of course, was a big thrill. I ran as hard as I could with several thousand other grim, silent marathoners through the streets of San Francisco in 1984. We went through Golden Gate Park. We went through Chinatown. We went up Market Street and finished at City Hall.

The only sound I uttered the entire race was a relieved grunt as I crossed the finish line. I had been so uptight during the race, my worst pain was in the crook of my elbow from holding my arms up too high. I must have looked like a Tyrannosaurus rex running down the street with my little arms up in front of me. And, of course, I never walked. At the water stops, I would grab a cup off the table, crumple it at the top, and suck it down, barely breaking stride, just like the front runners who actually had a reason to act like that. Every mile after mile 2 hurt. Every mile between mile 20 and mile 26 was hell on Earth and seemed to last for 10 years.

After the race, I collapsed on the grass, wrapped in a space blanket with my finisher's medal around my neck. I felt like I had been hit by a Mack truck. And what do you think was uppermost in my mind as I lay there after this first supreme, soul-fulfilling marathon effort, after having reached this sought after running landmark, this glorious pinnacle of human athletic endurance? I was thinking, *Hmm, I bet I could do better than 3:29.*

So I was launched into my marathon years, in which each spring, I would try my best to lower my marathon PR (personal record) from the year before. All the running I did between attempts was pointed toward this one goal, several months each year of tempo runs, interval workouts, hill repeats, and long runs done mostly over the same stretch of blacktop road.

In a good year, I would clip a couple of minutes off my best time and go home mildly satisfied. In a bad year, I would overrun the first half of the race and blow up when I hit the wall. Either way, my conclusion would be that if I just worked out more, I could have that breakthrough, transcendent race next year, and somehow I would be satisfied with my accomplishment. I was on a marathon treadmill. I kept seeing the same asphalt going by underneath my feet. I kept encountering the same walls around me even though I was outside and there were no walls.

ROCKY

Ironically, even before I took my first step in my first organized race, there was something right there that might have clued me in as to where I was going wrong. It was the *Rocky* theme music blasting out of the

speakers before the start. "Trying hard now…Getting strong now…
Gonna fly now…"

Rocky, the film written by and starring then largely unknown actor,
Sylvester Stallone, burst onto the scene in 1976. The film had such a
small budget that the famous scene where Rocky courts the painfully
shy Adrian, played by Talia Shire, at an ice skating rink was reworked
so the couple was there after closing because paying the extras to make
it appear as if the rink were open would have been too expensive.
The film garnered 10 Academy Award nominations and won in three
categories, including Best Picture. America couldn't resist the uplifting,
David versus Goliath, underdog-triumphing-over-all-odds story set in a
gritty working-class section of Philadelphia and Stallone's wry, honest,
clever portrayal of erstwhile loser Rocky Balboa.

The film opens with Rocky taking a pounding in the ring from a
washed-up prizefighter who looks like he's on his way to a win until
he resorts to a head butt. Rocky flies into a rage and dispatches his
opponent with a series of savage blows. Despite this win, it is clear no
one respects Rocky or expects anything from him. Nor does he believe
much in himself. When he drags a young girl away from a gang of street
toughs and tries to council her on proper behavior, she blows him off.
He walks away shaking his head and asks himself, "Who are you to
give advice, Creepo? Who are you?"

Back in the shambles of his tiny apartment, he lingers over a picture of
himself as a young boy, a boy presumably bright and full of promise,
and then he curls up all alone in bed with a handful of ice held up
against his slashed forehead, the picture of dashed hopes. Later at the
local gym, Rocky's trainer (Burgess Meredith) has moved Rocky out
of his locker, giving it to a more promising fighter, who chides Rocky,
"Hey, I dig your locker, man."

Rocky confronts the trainer about why he always treats him so poorly. "Cause you had the talent to become a good fighter," the trainer growls, "and instead of that you became a leg breaker for a cheap second-rate loan shark."

"It's a livin'," Rocky replies.

"It's a waste of life," the trainer shoots back.

It's clear that Rocky needs motivation and incentive, a goal to get him moving, so he can define himself as something other than a loser and a bum. And that's what goals are all about. Goal setting is a tremendously important process in life. It forces you to think about your future, what you want that future to be, and helps you define how to get there. Goals help you narrow down what activities are worth pursuing and what can be left behind as irrelevant to getting you where you want to go. They provide focus. They allow you to measure your progress, take pride in your accomplishments, and make the most of your efforts.

Of course, in the movie, fate intervenes to define Rocky's goal for him. He is selected to fight Apollo Creed, boxing's world champion, when a heavily promoted Fourth of July bout faces cancellation due to Creed's opponent injuring himself. Time is too short for a suitable replacement to be found, but Creed hits upon the idea of salvaging the match by giving a local fighter a chance at the title. He picks Rocky solely because of his flashy ring name, the Italian Stallion.

Rocky's goal, then, appears to be winning the fight or at least going the distance with the champion and remaining standing. But Rocky's problem is not that he needs to be the world boxing champion. His problem is that no one believes in him, and he doesn't believe in himself. His problem is that he has potential, but no will to pursue it.

Rocky's real goal, then, is to break out of his lethargy and live up to his potential.

The beauty of the film is that we get a good sense of Rocky's journey as he develops on the path toward his goal. On training day one, his alarm goes off at four o'clock in the morning. A radio announcer conveniently tells us it is 28 degrees Fahrenheit outside. We watch as, face totally impassive as usual, Rocky breaks five raw eggs into a glass and then, without hesitating, chugs it all down. Outside, he stretches briefly and then breaks into a painfully slow jog up the desolate street where he lives. When he reaches the Philadelphia Museum of Art, he can barely limp to the top of the frosty steps. An aching side stitch has him clinching one fist against his ribs. He is gasping for breath. And thus the journey begins, fraught with difficulty and seemingly unpromising.

Little by little we see the change come over Rocky. We see him gaining strength and confidence. We see his friends come around one by one, offering him support and respect. Even one of Apollo Creed's handlers sits up and takes notice as he watches Rocky on TV pounding a side of beef vigorously, demonstrating one of his training techniques for a local journalist. The interview ends as the camera focuses in on Rocky's blood splattered fists. "Hey, Champ," the handler calls to Creed. "Come look at this boy you're going to fight on TV. Looks like he means business."

"Yeah, yeah, I mean business, too," Creed flippantly responds, not looking at the TV, too busy to be bothered with thoughts of his pushover opponent.

Later we get a montage of scenes leading up to Rocky's triumphant return to the museum steps that wonderfully encapsulates his long journey to remake himself. It begins with Rocky jogging through a ravished area near some train tracks, carrying bricks in his hands for weights. Then, he's punching a bag, doing a series of one-armed push-ups, taking a series of blows to his midsection, hitting a slab of beef, and then back to the push-ups with his jazzed-up trainers offering encouragement. He's jogging through a market with a smile on his face, comfortably in control of his pace. Someone throws him an apple. Along the waterfront, he speeds up into an impressive sprint, and then, finally, we see him bounding up the steps of the art museum, taking them three and four at a time, reaching the top with no undue strain.

Here is the heart of the movie. Rocky runs up the stairs and then turns and thrusts his arms into the air triumphantly with the city spread out beneath his feet and the theme song reaching a crescendo. This is the moment when Rocky achieves the real goal that he has pursued. It's the moment when he knows he has reached his full potential, the moment when he believes fully in himself.

What follows, the fight, is in many ways essentially irrelevant. True, during the fight Rocky is able to demonstrate his incredible determination and courage, but these things result from the transformation that Rocky worked on during his training. In the end, something that many people who saw the film probably don't even remember correctly, Rocky does not win the fight. Most will remember Rocky standing in the ring terribly bloodied and yelling for Adrian, but as for the fight, it was scored as a draw, and, therefore, Apollo Creed won and remained champion.

FOCUS ON THE JOURNEY

In a very similar vein, when you set and pursue a goal in running, it is not achieving the particular time or finishing the particular distance that is the point, but rather, the changes you effect in yourself while pursuing the goal. My problem in my early days of running was that I was always focused on the outcome and not the journey to get there. Everything I thought about my running and, to some extent, about myself had to do with how the race came out. If I didn't break my previous time, it put a shadow on everything I'd done during my training. If I did lower my time, I'd still feel some disappointment in not lowering it even more. I had it all backwards. What I needed to be thinking about was what the running was doing for me as a whole.

Just think about the journey you make when you set completing a marathon for the first time as your running goal. You go from a runner who has never run more than six or seven miles at a stretch to a runner who can expect to last the entire 26-plus miles of a marathon. You gradually build your strength and stamina. You drop the extra pounds. You develop discipline. Your perspective shifts. You learn to get out the door to get those extra miles in even when you might feel like doing something else. You take on those long runs, learn that you are capable of much more than you ever thought possible, and, as the miles pile up, you learn to summon the courage and determination it takes to finish the run on tired and dead legs. All the focus on running tends to shift your perspective away from your problems. You feel less stressed every day. You feel good about your efforts, especially getting through those long weekend runs, and your self-esteem gets a major boost.

When you finish that last long training run before the marathon, you are on top of the world, like Rocky on the museum steps. Here is the moment you have been striving for, when you are ready to go to the starting line prepared for what is to come. The race itself should be like the icing on the cake. Think of it as your reward. On race day, you should relax, knowing that you have put in the time and effort to be equal to the challenge. Ironically, the more you are able to relax and just let the race take care of itself and the less you worry about the outcome, the more likely you are to give your best performance.

Also consider this. You may spend six long months getting prepared for that marathon. The race lasts just one morning. Spend the six months trying to enjoy the process of running. Marvel in the sensations you are feeling and note the changes you perceive in how your body is adjusting to the extra training. Pay attention to your surroundings. Get out to new places for your runs and get lost in the experience. Don't focus on the forest, that is, the end goal of running the marathon, to the extent that you are blind to all the fabulous trees that you're passing along the way, the stands of aspens with their leaves fluttering in the breeze, the mighty oaks shading the path, the fragrant pine trees, the laurels, the brightly colored maples, and the awe-inspiring redwoods.

Along with your ultimate goal, think in terms of lots of mini goals. Each day's run is a goal in itself. Every time you conquer a run, you have overcome the inertia that keeps others on the couch. You have done something for yourself and for your health, both mental and physical.

Some days the goal might be to just breeze through a few easy miles. On other days, your workout might present a whole series of goals. Get through the fifth of six half-mile intervals in a certain time. Go up the hill one more time in your hill repeats. Maintain the tempo in your tempo run for one more mile. Surge to that farthest telephone pole in your fartlek pick-up. Narrow your focus down to that single goal you have at the moment and then pursue that goal with all the passion in your being. Everything else in life is shut out for a while as you lose yourself in this singular pursuit. Pursuing a goal passionately is liberating and exhilarating, and running gives you that opportunity all the time, not just when you're racing.

Remember your goal isn't necessarily to get through the forest but to enjoy all the fabulous trees along the way.

© Gary Dudney

In my earlier days of running, I never paid any attention to the process of running. I was too worried about what would happen on race day. In the film, we see Rocky's journey. At one point he breaks off from his one-armed push-ups, relaxes on his elbow, and smiles at the trainer. It's the first smile we get out of Stallone in the whole movie. It's a moment when we see him appreciating what he is doing and sharing the feeling with his friend. If later, during the big fight, Apollo Creed were to knock him out in the first round, he would still have that moment of knowing he had done his best and had reached his full potential.

CHAPTER 4

CHASING LEADVILLE

Leadville, Colorado, sits in the Rocky Mountains at an altitude of 10,200 feet in the open plain of the Arkansas River Valley, isolated and alone. It's the highest incorporated city in the United States of America and the only official town in Lake County. Almost half the county's residents live there. It started as a silver mining boomtown in 1877; once it was second in size only to Denver with a population of 40,000 (now 2,600) and hosted a parade of Wild West figures and mine swindlers until the silver profits went bust with the repeal of the Sherman Silver Purchase Act in 1893. Thereafter, miners turned their attention to the lead and zinc that had always been there but had played second fiddle to the silver. The Second World War sparked a demand for molybdenum, which, it turned out, Leadville had in abundance, at one time producing 75 percent of the world's supply.

In spite of the pizzazz and dazzle that molybdenum mining brought to the town, Leadville wilted back to its Old West roots and presents itself today as a not too prosperous place but with a dusty, dog-eared charm. It has a rambling collection of creaky Victorian buildings that show their age like distressed antiques. The row of 19th-century storefronts on Harrison Street still conjures up the kind of place that the Badman from Bodie might ride into and shoot up.

Standing on the corner in the center of town under an intense summer sun that is microwaving everything in its path, I half expect a grizzled old miner to sidle up to me, spit a stream of *terbakky* into a cuspidor, and in a high squeaky voice say, "Lookee here, Pardner. This'n here town don't cotton to no sidewinders, no way, no how." The air is so thin, just walking around window shopping for tourist junk in the curio shops, I have to stop and catch my breath every few minutes. Off on the horizon, Mt. Elbert and Mt. Massive sit brooding and ominous. They are Colorado's two highest peaks in a state that is known for high peaks.

The snowmelt from the surrounding mountains feed the headwaters of the Arkansas River which flows south from Leadville and then makes a grand turn out of the mountains to the east. The Arkansas (pronounced AR-kan-saw here and in the state of Arkansas, but ar-KAN-zes when it crosses Kansas) then meanders for a thousand miles through the Great Plains, flowing eventually through Wichita, Kansas, Tulsa, Oklahoma, and Little Rock, Arkansas, before finally emptying into the Mississippi River. I peer down the length of Harrison Street, and it strikes me that the snow that melted off the rooftops I'm seeing right now might have ended up in my drinking water in Wichita when I was a kid. Was Leadville calling to me even back then? Did the place already have a claim on me?

Perhaps. Follow running long enough and deeply enough and passionately enough, and you might just end up like me in Leadville in August under this glaring sun facing one of running's toughest challenges, the Leadville Trail 100, "The Race Across the Sky." It seems like Leadville can't be avoided. It's a long-distance runner's destiny. Say the word "Leadville" over and over. It sounds like an elephantine iron bell tolling out a death knell, and, if you're a runner, well, sorry, it tolls for thee.

The average elevation of the course is over 10,000 feet. The high point, the top of Hope Pass, is at 12,600 feet. You go there twice. And just for good measure, the time limit for Leadville is set at a miserly 30 hours. Miss the mark by a second, and you are not a finisher. You might as well have stayed home in Akron and had a barbeque. Other tough, mountainous 100-mile races allow up to 34 or 36 hours for an official finish. At Leadville, after 30 hours, you get the boot. In a typical year, less than half the starters in the race reach the finish.

The race was the brainchild of Ken Chlouber, a rough-edged ex-miner and Colorado state senator who lost his job when the molybdenum mine temporarily closed and threw Leadville's economy into a tailspin. Chlouber reasoned that the audacious challenge of a 100-mile race would draw visitors from around the country and boost Leadville's flagging fortunes. It worked. Like the Western States Endurance Run, the idea of toughing out such a gargantuan effort appealed to the type of runners who live to see limits pushed and the impossible, well, *possible*.

The hospital director in Leadville didn't believe human beings could run 100 miles at such an altitude without someone dying. In that dire prediction, Chlouber saw a silver lining. "At least that'll make us famous," he is said to have replied, or words to that effect.

It's August 16, 2002. The 20th running of the Leadville Trail 100 is tomorrow. I'm standing in front of the Sixth Street Gym just a few steps from the corner of Sixth and Harrison where the race will begin. The dilapidated gym is an odd hunk of a building. No entry way, steps, fancy columns, porch, overhang, vestibule, balcony, or awning interrupt the way it squats directly on the sidewalk. Gray stucco clings to its facade. The aqua blue paint on the window and doorframes brighten it up a bit, but it is a lost cause.

From the sidewalk, you step through a narrow door into a small room that looks like a large shower stall. From there you enter the gym proper and encounter an interior space that continues the themes from the exterior. The floor is chipped, marred, faded, and blotched with big brown stains as if the place were used to slaughter sheep in the off season. The walls are adorned with all manner of mismatched panels that must have been taken from various demolition sites. Barren steel girders crisscross overhead. Old parachutes hang from the girders. They may once have been bright and silky white, but now they're discolored to a dull yellow and covered with forlorn patches.

THE WISDOM OF CHLOUBER

Shabby as it is, though, today this place is the epicenter of endurance running in the United States. The little gym is crowded to bursting. People hang over the narrow balcony that rings the court, hooting and hollering like a rowdy crowd in a saloon waiting for the dancin' girls. Chlouber is prowling around the front of the room dressed in the most garish running shorts you can imagine. He brings out two stools and eyes one of them suspiciously. He puts it on the ground sideways and stomps on it. Satisfied, he sets it back upright. Chlouber is tall and rangy. His long, unruly hair, massive forehead, craggy face, and gravelly voice make him seem every bit the former miner that he is. From his very first words, which he shouts into the microphone, everyone is mesmerized by him. "ARE YOU READY? ARE YOU READY?"

"We've got runners here from 44 states," he says. After a long pause, "From four foreign countries." Another long pause. "And from AR-KAN-SAW," contempt dripping from his voice. Everyone laughs. A girl sitting on the floor at Chlouber's feet is stretching, pulling her leg impossibly high up across her chest. Two big dogs next to her wag their tails and lick her face.

From where I'm sitting, I can see Chlouber's notes, a confused mess of scribbles on a piece of notebook paper. Co-race director, Merilee O'Neil, a stocky woman with long silver hair, stands at his elbow, whispering in his ear and directing him to the next item on his list. Chlouber mumbles and breathes heavily into the mike. It's getting warm in the gym. He tells someone in the back to open the door. "You might have to kick it," he adds. In going over the rules, he says only one pacer is allowed per runner, except for the final mile or so. For that, he says, "We don't care if you bring your whole first-grade class along." He fields a question about using walking sticks. "Ain't no rule against 'em," he says, "but they're just plain stupid."

He gets to the meat of his talk. "Now I know you're all waiting for the pep talk, but this is no pep talk or motivational speech or sales talk or whatever. This is truth, just plain truth." The audience is now leaning forward, leaning into his words. He utters his iconic statement, "You're better than you think you are; you can do more than you think you can."

"The truth," he continues, "is that inside every one of us there is an inexhaustible well of strength, power, grit, and determination. You *can* finish. So I am asking you to do one thing. Do not quit. What is the number one reason people quit? Because they say it hurts." He smirks at that notion. "Well, I guarantee you that if you keep going, it will hurt no more than 30 hours. If you quit, it will hurt for the next 365 days. People will have one question for you after this race: 'Did you finish?' Now you can either say, 'Yes, I did.' Or you can spend the next 15 minutes dreaming up some lame excuse."

"Make pain your friend," he continues, "and you will never be alone." I turn that over in my mind, thinking maybe being alone from time to time wouldn't be so bad. Pain, determination, grit—these are all great concepts sitting here the day before the race. I wonder how well these things will work out on the trail the next day and night. Dr. John Perna, the race's medical director, offers some more concrete advice: "Pee yellow, bad; pee clear, good."

We pile out of the Sixth Street Gym with everyone all charged up, me more than anyone. *Wow*, I'm thinking, *I have an inexhaustible well of determination and grit. I can do more than I think I can. I don't have to fear pain; I just have to make friends with it. I'm not going to quit because I'll be damned if I'm going to end up as one of those poor souls who has to duck his head and explain why he didn't finish.* I wanted to hug Chlouber, the big galoot! He'd set me straight. I felt like I was on fire; of course, the sun in the open street baking my head might have had something to do with that.

But one idea kept troubling me. Almost every year at Leadville more than half the runners quit. What happened to their inexhaustible wells? Wasn't pain their friend, too? These were troubling questions and didn't fit in with the enormous confidence I now felt about my chances to finish the race and take home a silver Leadville belt buckle. This idea about reaching down into the well when things got bad and tapping into all that grit and determination just seemed so foolproof. I decided I had nothing to worry about.

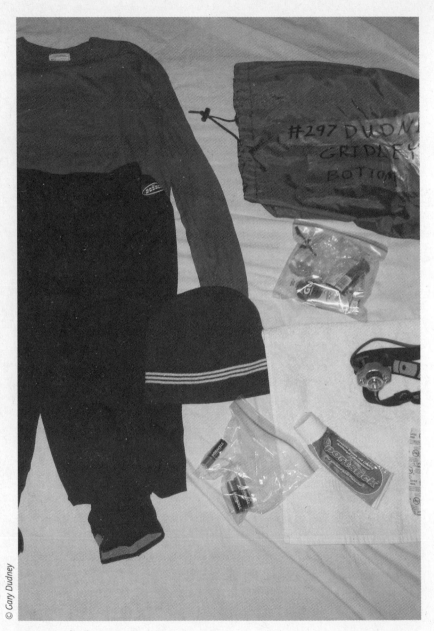

Standard stuff for a 100-mile race

Nevertheless, that night I barely slept. Chlouber's words churned through my mind, mixed with fear, mixed with the knowledge that I had to get up impossibly early to make the 4 a.m. start. Plus, every few minutes I woke up gasping for air and had to hyperventilate to give my brain sufficient oxygen so that I could continue to live on this planet. I was about to undergo a great learning experience. Running was about to substitute all these notions about what I could accomplish with some hard reality.

Maybe I was asleep when the alarm rang at three o'clock, maybe not. I tore myself out of bed and began the process of covering myself with sunblock, skin lubricant, bug spray, and strategically placed Band-Aids. I laced up my running shoes and put on a fancy lightweight jacket with warm cap and gloves ready in the pockets. I filled my running bottles with tap water, put on my waist belt with the side pockets for the bottles, adjusted the strap, and looked at myself in the mirror. I looked ready and terrified.

RABBIT RUN

Outside in the dark the air was thin and cold. Four hundred runners shifted around uneasily, jumping up and down to keep warm, their arms wrapped tightly around them. A bright lamp on a pole near the starting line threw a harsh light over the street. Jerking, elongated shadows danced over the pavement. I cowered, shivering under a bush and then joined the other runners on the street with five minutes to go. I recited the Lord's Prayer to myself. I felt like I was already reaching down into my well of determination. After all, I was more than happy to make pain my friend and tough it out, but that was assuming I'd had a good night's sleep and felt warm and comfortable. Maybe there was more to this than I realized. The long sweep of Sixth Street heading out of town was before us. A shotgun went off and scared the living bejesus out of me. I took off like a spooked rabbit.

We ran out of town and got onto a wide jeep road called the Boulevard. Dust kicked up by the runners in front of me hung thick in the air illuminated by a dozen bouncing flashlight beams. I calmed down now that I was moving and actually getting something done and concentrated on not turning an ankle on the larger rocks strewn about the road. By the time we reached the single track that skirted the edge of Turquoise Lake, I'd discovered that my elevated heart rate and faster tempo of breathing from the running was giving me sufficient oxygen to keep me going steadily. I just had to keep my pace under control because whenever I sped up I'd get behind the curve and start gasping for air.

The single track along Turquoise Lake was a minefield of rocks and roots. A string of lights bounced along the lake shore before me and behind me. Occasionally the dark just around me was interrupted by a camper shining a flashlight. We streamed through a shouting, yelling pack of crew people at Tabor Boat Ramp and then were immediately back on the dark trail. It was quiet. The only sounds were the grunts and heavy breathing of the other runners as we worked our way over all the obstacles. Between having to concentrate on not tripping and the early hour and the weight of the task before us, the talking and joking that had gone on back on the Boulevard had all died out.

Light rose slowly over the lake. A thick mist hung over the water. I could see the forest on the opposite shore now and the hulk of Sugarloaf Pass which we would be climbing shortly. Up around a bend in the shoreline were the lights of the May Queen Aid Station, which was placed a full half marathon (13.5 miles) from the start. It was not lost on me that half-marathoners would already be just about finished with their race while here at Leadville we hadn't even reached the first aid station and had barely scratched the surface of the race proper.

At May Queen, we were processed through a large tent that was open at each end. Inside, heaters were going full blast. I passed by an array of food, filled up my water bottles, and then checked my number out as I emerged from the other end of the tent. *Bam, bam*, and I was back out on the Colorado Trail in a forest of lodge pole pines and aspens. Boulders were scattered everywhere. Streams cut across the trail. I ran in stutter steps over a constantly shifting jumble of big rocks and downed trees. It was tiring work, and I found I had to take it slowly or I immediately started gasping for air.

Next came the first major climb—a trek over Sugarloaf Pass, but the way up was on a wide, gently sloped jeep road. The sun had crept a little way up into the sky, so runners were shedding jackets and long-sleeved shirts and tying them around their waists. The summit was anti-climactic. The road just flattened out and then bent down. From the road, we turned into a wide swath that had been cleared in the forest to build a power line. The massive power lines cracked and hissed above us as we descended to an asphalt road at the bottom that took us to the Fish Hatchery Aid Station.

There I received some bad news. Back home at sea level, I had put together what I thought was a conservative pace chart that would get me to the finish in a comfortable 29 hours and 30 minutes, leaving me a half-hour safety margin before the 30-hour cutoff. I'd checked my progress against the plan at May Queen and found I was a little behind schedule, but not by much. Since May Queen, I'd been pushing it, trying to find the sweet spot where I was running as hard as I could without getting into oxygen debt. It felt like I was whacking away at the Leadville monster, keeping myself together, strategizing, and reaching down into my well of grit and determination. Wouldn't Chlouber be nodding with satisfaction at this tenderfoot? But at the Fish Hatchery, I got a cold shower. I had fallen even further behind my race plan than I was before.

I was feeling a little dazed as I picked over the food inside the big maintenance shed building that housed the aid station. Volunteers suggested sandwiches, energy bars, potato chips, or chunks of baked potatoes dipped in a bowl of salt. My worried expression seemed to be sparking their concern. "Looking good," one of them lied to me. I smiled wanly.

I stepped out of the shed, hitched up my running shorts, and vowed to kill the next section of the course, which by Leadville standards looked like something manageable—a long, flat, paved road that curved around through a valley followed by a gentle climb up a fire road to the Halfmoon Aid Station. I figured I was finally going to put the big kibosh on my pace problem and get back on track. Leadville apparently thought otherwise. Even though I was down under 10,000 feet at that point on the course, each stride seemed sluggish and labored. I couldn't keep up with runners who were just barely jogging along in front of me. I would lose my breath and need to walk a stretch. Then when I started up again, it was with the same dead leg shuffle that was the best effort I could manage.

By the time I reached Halfmoon, I'd lost even more margin against my race plan. It began to dawn on me that I was in trouble. Between Halfmoon and the next aid station at Twin Lakes was another punishing section of the Colorado Trail featuring a series of three major climbs. The first two climbs culminated in false summits where you swore you'd reached the top and were heading back down only to find another uphill in your path. I tried to hang on to a pair of women negotiating the trail with walking sticks that clicked endlessly against the rocks along the trail, but they soon dropped me, and the clicking faded out ahead of me.

HOPELESS PASS

At Twin Lakes, 40 miles, I sat down on an ice chest with my head bowed. I was afraid to look up at Hope Pass, the next and greatest obstacle on the course. My race plan was shot to hell, and only the thought of slinking back home without having even set foot on Hope Pass kept me from quitting right there. I guessed that now was really the time to be grubbing around in my well of determination, but the well seemed to have gone missing. I wasn't afraid to take on a little pain, either, but this wasn't so much pain as just the pure inability to keep putting one foot in front of the other. It was too late to get better trained. It was too late to be a stronger runner. I had to work with what I had, but it didn't seem to be enough no matter how much I wanted it to be. Chlouber hadn't covered that.

I joylessly gathered my supplies, adjusted my running belt, and trudged on with the vague idea that maybe things would change for the better. I crossed the knee-deep river that flows through the broad meadow just beyond Twin Lakes. A guy next to me was walking across with his feet stuck in trash bags. "Does that keep your feet dry?" I asked. "I'll let you know in about five steps," he said.

I reached the trees on the other side of the meadow and looked up the trail that had to be climbed to reach Hope Pass. My heart sunk. It was a steep, rocky single track that cut straight up the mountain. The trail designers must have missed all the classes at trail-making school about switchbacks and gentle grades. The Rocky Mountains were working overtime here to supply the rocks. The smoothest parts of the trail were gardens of half-buried rocks; the worst parts of the trail looked like Brobdingnagian staircases.

I leaned into the climb and hadn't gotten far when I heard someone shouting from above, "Runner up! Runner up!" I looked up to see Chad Ricklefs, who was enjoying a turn as one of the top ultrarunners in the country, barreling down the trail, coming at me like a freight train, rushing over the tricky footing as if it were nothing. His pacer was frantically bringing up the rear, barely able to hang on to him. Another runner, Hal Koerner, who'd finished second here the year before, rushed past just a few seconds later hot on Ricklefs' heels. It was difficult for me to believe that these guys and I were somehow participating in the same event. They were impossibly far ahead of me. I'd just left 40 miles. They were about to hit 60.

Halfway up the trail, before the forest began petering out at timberline, I started encountering runners sitting on logs or rocks next to the trail, elbows propped on their knees, heads down. "You okay," I'd ask.

"Restin'," they'd reply or just nod their heads to save the energy it took to power their vocal chords. It wasn't long before I was seeking out my own log. Resting suddenly seemed like a powerfully good idea.

I sat down with my back to the slope, feeling an enormous inertia settle over me. I was sitting for maybe five minutes when a woman leading a llama appeared and offered me a soft drink. She was using the llama to pack supplies up to the aid station. I'd read that llamas were used here for that purpose but to have the tall beast standing next to me placidly gazing about the forest and bearing soft drinks seemed to strain the boundaries of reality. The strangeness of it all got me back on my feet and all the way to the Hope Pass Aid Station. There I found a lot of other llamas scattered over the meadow, chewing up grass and ignoring the desperate human beings like me who were staggering around like zombies.

© Gary Dudney

Just a few of the rocks you'll find along the Colorado Trail in the aptly named Rocky Mountains.

After trying some soup at the aid station, I pushed myself up to the top of the pass where I noted the Tibetan prayer flags strung out over the rocks. I was sure they had been put there with good intentions, but for me, they conjured up the Death Zone on Mt. Everest, not exactly what I wanted to be thinking right then. I stumbled down the other side of Hope Pass and took the measure of the runners coming back up from the turnaround some five miles away. They seemed tired but determined, apparently accessing their wells of grit. They made way for the runners coming down so they could take the opportunity to lean over and rest for a few seconds, hands on knees. I got to the bottom of the trail and turned up the road for the 3-mile run to Winfield, the 50-mile mark of the race and the turnaround for home. I knew I needed to make up some time, but the slight uphill grade of the road was too much for me. I picked out a tree, did a little shuffle jog until I reached it, and then walked until I felt human again. Over and over.

I finally turned into what was billed as the "ghost town" of Winfield, but it was nothing more than an odd collection of modern outbuildings with corrugated roofs. Swinging saloon doors, hitching posts, and tumbleweed rolling down Main Street were nowhere to be found. One larger shed served as the aid station, and I had no sooner reached it than I found myself collapsed into a camp chair, my waist belt in the dirt at my feet.

I prayed that I was way over the cutoff time, which at Winfield was an elapsed time of 14 hours, so that there was no question of continuing. At 14 hours, you only had 16 hours to get all the way back to Leadville. That meant that on legs that had already passed through the meat grinder of the first 50 miles of the course, you were going to run through the dark of night over 10 million rocks, exhausted from having had no sleep, and do that somehow only two hours slower than it took you to get out to Winfield on fresh legs in the daylight.

THE ICEMAN COMETH

The aid station captain approached me. He was the one who had the power to cut off the little plastic armband that had been on my wrist since I checked into the race the day before. "You're a little past the cutoff time," he said, "about six minutes. But you know what? You can rest here for a moment and get yourself something to eat. Just take your time, and I'll let you go on. You can still make it, Buddy."

I looked up at him, hoping maybe he was kidding. He didn't look like he was kidding. I didn't want this to be my decision. I wanted the full, heavy weight of the race rules to crash over me like a big wave and wash me out to sea where I could be left to drown in peace. I'd missed the cutoff, so wasn't that it? No ifs, ands, or buts.

Chlouber's words rang in my ears, "…an inexhaustible well…don't quit…you can do more than you think you can." It all rang hollow. I felt so incredibly bad. It hurt so much. I was convinced I felt worse than everybody else in the race. In years to come I would find out that that was not true, that everyone else felt just as bad as I did, that I had no lock on the suffering, but right there at that moment in Winfield in that camp chair, it seemed to me like the truest thing on Earth.

I lifted my arm up in the air and said, "Cut it off."

"That's your wristwatch," the aid station captain said. "Give me your other arm." I lifted the correct arm, and he snipped off my plastic armband. I had DNFed (Did Not Finish).

FINISH LINE

The next morning, as ten o'clock approached, the last of the finishers were coming up Sixth Street. I stood watching from the curb, all showered and rested. I was telling myself that almost everyone has suffered through a DNF at Leadville. It almost seemed like a requisite part of learning what it takes to make it through this race. Way off in the distance, the remaining runners and their pacers appeared as tiny figures coming up over a rise about a half mile away. From there they had to run down into a valley and up to the finish over a carpet placed on the street. It took about 10 minutes to negotiate that final stretch. Because it was unusually hot that year, the finish percentage was below average, just 41 percent. Six out of every ten runners who thought they were ready, like me, failed.

Of course, I had the extra burden of knowing that I could have kept going. I hadn't suffered a "mechanical." I hadn't timed way out. I had quit, in spite of all that Chlouber had had to say on the subject. I had quit, period.

I watched each finisher as they came across the line. Merilee O'Neil was there to slip a ribbon with a finisher's medallion over their heads. Then she gave each runner a hug. Afterward, the runner would spend just a moment being congratulated by friends and family before lying down on the concrete or collapsing on the curb. At the end of other races, you'd see finishers walking around, standing in groups and laughing, grazing picnic tables for food. Not at Leadville. Almost everyone immediately after finishing ended up on their backs.

I couldn't imagine what these runners had gone through to get back here over those last 50 miles. I had found out there was a world of difference between understanding all those concepts that Chlouber had talked about and actually executing on them. Knowing you had a deep well of determination was not the same thing as knowing how to use that deep well of determination to keep going when things went to hell on you.

But there was one thing I did know for sure that morning surrounded by all those prostrate runners. I had to come back. I had to cross the Leadville finish line myself someday. I had to hug Merilee O'Neil.

CHAPTER 5

STAYING
RELENTLESSLY POSITIVE

Quitting at Leadville really bugged me. Back home, comfortably in bed, and recovered from the trauma of dragging myself over 50 miles of mountainous terrain at 10,000 feet, I was deeply into second guessing my decision.

Sure, I'd been exhausted sitting in that camp chair in Winfield. The relief of getting off my feet and the lure of just instantly ending the whole struggle had been overwhelming. My feet had been exquisitely painful, my legs were dead, and I had zero energy, but then what had I expected? Was I going to waltz over a 100 miles of rocky trail up there in the sky, trot up to the finish line, and then collect a coveted silver finisher's buckle without getting into any major pain and discomfort?

It was clear I didn't have a workable strategy for when the chips were really down, but I had this sneaking suspicion that I hadn't been totally finished in that chair. I was now, however, one of those lost souls who had to duck his head and root around in the mind cellar for the least damaging excuse for why I'd quit.

THE NIGHT ABOVE PASADENA

What really bothered me was that in the past I'd managed to resurrect myself from dire circumstances. In my very first attempt at running 100 miles in 1997 at the Angeles Crest 100, which passes through the Angeles National Forest near Los Angeles, starting in the town of Wrightwood on the eastern slopes of the San Gabriel Mountains and ending in Pasadena in the west, something remarkable had happened.

It had been an eventful day. A group of Tarahumara runners were up from Mexico to be part of the race. Many of them were wearing rough-looking sandals and big, billowy orange shirts. They were fueling up with some odd concoction and were ushered in and out of the aid stations with drums and flute music. As diverting as they were, though, they had no effect on the day getting hotter and hotter, which, despite months of hard training on my part, left me dragging along through the afternoon desperately trying to keep my brain from bursting into flames.

When evening finally descended, I couldn't wait to get into some cooler air and start layering on all the warm clothes I had waiting for me in my drop bags along the course. I figured a nice brisk night would be invigorating and just what I needed to perk me back up. But as the night wore on, the temperatures down in the stuffy canyons we were running through hardly moderated at all. The night air was warm and stifling. I never put a thing on over the t-shirt I'd been wearing all day, and I was still sweating.

The heat wasn't helping my thinking skills. My pacer and I had just come around the back end of a narrow canyon when I saw a couple of runners kneeling in the brush next to the trail. They were shining their lights down over the side of the canyon, and I heard one of them say to the other, "You see it, don't you?"

"Yeah," the other guy said. "It's a cougar. You can see its eyes."

The little scene was so surprising to me and passed by so quickly as we ran along that it was quite a while before I realized what had just happened. "Wow," I finally said to my pacer, "those guys were looking at a cougar."

"What guys?" my pacer asked.

"The guys we just passed," I said. "One of 'em said there was a cougar."

"Yeah, okay," my pacer said and then asked me how long it had been since I had my last energy gel packet.

Later that night, I was surprised to see other runners stretched out on the ground next to the trail. They looked like dead people. Now, had I been in a normal frame of mind, the fact that I had just seen two guys, who my pacer hadn't seen at all, discussing a cougar and that there were possibly dead people lying along the trail would have been quite upsetting to me. But in my muddled consciousness, I think the most coherent thought I had was, *Oh boy, there are sure strange things going on in the San Gabriel Mountains at night.*

The longest, hardest climb of the race started at mile 75 at an aid station called Chantry Flats. It was a gain of 3,100 feet done over six miles of unbroken ascent. For me, this treasure came in the middle of the night, and it was crushing. I started the climb feeling like I was at the end of my rope, so by the time we were near the top I was ready to, oh I don't know, never run another step as long as I lived.

The road we were on climbed up to a ridge. After having been in deep, uninhabited wilderness all day and most of the night, we looked down off the ridge at the million dazzling lights of Pasadena spread out at our feet stretching up and down the coast as far as the eye could see. As awe inspiring as this sight was, though, the impression faded quickly when I looked to my right and saw that the next section of trail we had to face was more uphill that climbed along the ridge toward the top of Mt. Wilson. I had thought we were finished with the climb.

Without thinking it over or even realizing what I was doing, I sat down and said to myself, *I'm done.* I didn't know how I was going to get off the mountain or what in the world was going to happen to me next, but I knew that I was all through with trying to run a 100 miles. I had gotten this far, but nothing in heaven or on earth was going to get me to go any farther. I had tried, but I had failed, simple as that.

 "Good idea," my pacer said, trying to convince me that I hadn't just thrown in the towel, "rest up for a while, then we'll get going. I'll time you. Five minutes."

I had nothing to say to that. *Let him time me all he wants,* I thought. *I'm staying here. I'm done.*

A few minutes passed, and then I started to hear voices. It was a group of runners coming up the same road I had just ascended a few minutes ago. There were six of them—four women and two men, probably three racers and three pacers.

They were talking in excited voices and laughing, having a grand old time. When they saw the lights of Pasadena, they screamed with delight. They stepped around me and trotted light-footed on up the trail. I watched them bounce away, still laughing. They were as carefree and happy as clams, delighted to be out in the woods at night, delighted with each other, delighted with life in general.

I sat there in my very deep funk, watching them skip away, and suddenly I became very angry. I was mad at those Bozos who were having such a good time while I was miserable as hell. I was mad at the course for putting this impossible climb right in the worst part of the run. I was mad at myself for being a quitter. I was filled up and bursting with anger. Again, almost without thinking, I jumped to my feet and started up the trail.

The incredibly strong emotions were wiping out all other thoughts and sensations in my mind. My exhaustion had evaporated, replaced probably by a healthy shot of adrenaline triggered by my anger. My legs were sore but more than up to the task of power walking to the top of the hill. The road crested, and we turned down toward the final aid station and the last stretch of trail before the finish. I never had another moment's hesitation and eventually limped across a grassy lawn under the finish banner to capture my first 100-mile belt buckle.

But what worked that night at Angles Crest was no strategy; it was just an emotional response unique to that moment and those circumstances. My experience at Leadville of having no answer as to how to rescue myself once the real hurting began was more the norm.

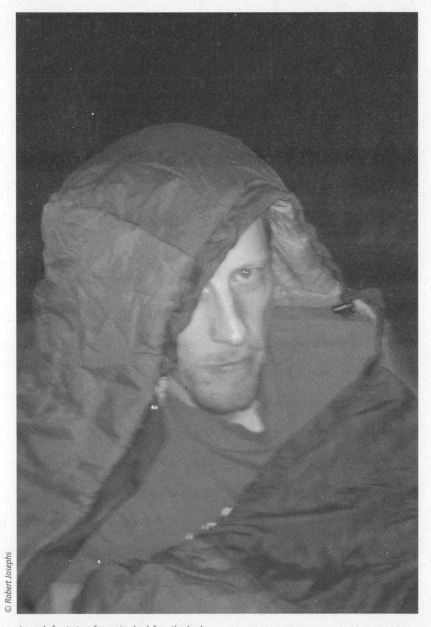

© Robert Josephs

In need of a strategy for coming back from the dead.

JOANN DAHLKOETTER

Nowadays I do have an effective strategy for dealing with pain and discomfort, and getting that strategy all started when I met JoAnn Dahlkoetter at the expo of the Big Sur International Marathon. She was sitting behind a pile of her books, *Your Performing Edge,* at a table, smiling at the runners who were passing by. I picked up a copy and turned it over. On the back it said, "Align Your Performance with the Vision in Your Heart." *Okay,* I thought, *that sounds good.*

Truth be told, I was quite thrilled to just meet a real live author who had written a real live book. That had never happened to me before. Given the prospect of her personally signing a copy of the book that I was going to take home and put on my own bookshelf, I think I would have bought a book from her entitled *This Is the Most Worthless Book You'll Ever Read.* We chatted for a moment. I gave her a check, and she wrote in my copy of the book, "To Gary, May the many miles of life be good to you." As it turned out, what I learned from that book actually *caused* the many miles of life to be good to me. That book changed my running completely.

There was nothing in any of the book's 256 pages about physical training for running. It all had to do with the mental side of things—in other words, how to *think* about running. And the message in a nutshell was: Keep things positive; avoid the negative. It was a simple, even an obvious, lesson, but as I was to learn, critically important.

I adapted many of Dahlkoetter's techniques to my running, but perhaps the most consequential was her advice to associate the pain and discomfort of a hard run with giving your best effort or performing up to your potential. It's natural to associate pain and struggling with something going wrong, with having a problem. Dahlkoetter's technique is to recognize the pain and discomfort as something that is natural, something to expect when you're trying hard. The pain is not an indication something is wrong; it is, in fact, telling you that you're doing well, that you're putting out your maximum effort, that you're living up to your training and reaching for your goal.

So the very feelings that would normally spark anxiety and put me on the path to panic were transformed, as if by magic, into something positive. It was like Jaws from the James Bond series had me boxed into a corner and was rushing at me full speed, his steel teeth bared. But the instant before he slammed into me and turned me into a grease spot, I pivoted just enough to avoid him, placed my hand on the back of his neck as he rushed by, and used all his momentum and the strength in my arm to crash him headlong into the wall behind me. It was like jiu jitsu. I learned how to turn all that enervating pain and discomfort into something positive.

Pain or any other unpleasant feeling, of course, must be acknowledged. You can't simply ignore it. Dahlkoetter would have you focus on it, even dwell on it for a little while, giving it its full due. But then you shift your focus elsewhere, like on your breathing or on your foot striking the ground. Register the pain as a normal part of the process, an indication of how hard you're running, and then let it fade into the background.

It's also a big help to realize that you're not alone in experiencing the painful demands of a long, hard run. Other runners will mask their stress and discomfort. I do the same thing. I may be a basket case inside with a million negative thoughts shooting through my head, but if a volunteer at an aid station asks me how I'm doing, I'll say with a breezy smile, "Never better." In fact, all the runners in a race around you are probably feeling just as badly as you are or worse, so really the pain is a shared thing. It's not just you. Take comfort in the fact that if they can handle it, so can you.

Dahlkoetter also advises runners to replace negative thoughts with some kind of positive affirmation. Replace, "My quads are shot," with "I felt this same way the last time I ran a PR." Replace, "I still have 10 miles to go," with "I've got 16 miles behind me, and it's less than 10 miles to the finish." Put a positive spin on anything going on around you. If another runner passes you by, imagine that you are drawing energy from that runner, which you can use to stay on his or her tail. If you're in a line of runners, a train, relax and imagine that you are streaming along with everybody else with little effort on your part. If you're going uphill, imagine a force pulling you to the top. On a downhill slope, imagine gravity doing all the work while you rest and just float down effortlessly. Creating these images of running strongly in your mind will translate into the real thing. Dahlkoetter also encourages you to keep in mind that you should celebrate your being able to push yourself so hard. It's not a sentence or a punishment; it's a source of pride, and it's an opportunity. You're healthy and active enough to be able to do this. You're one of the lucky ones.

Breaking down the race or the run into smaller chunks and avoiding thinking about the whole distance left to go is another technique for staying positive. As you reach each intermediate goal, give yourself credit for having conquered that segment of the race. Then focus on the next segment and keep your mind off how long it will be before you finish. If a goal like the next aid station starts to seem distant, work on just getting to the end of the next mile, or pick a tree in the distance and run that far.

In a similar vein, keep your focus on the here and now as you're running along. Let the time or distance goals you may have or the end of the race take care of itself. Those goals are best served by you doing the best thing for you at each moment of the run, anyway. Pay attention to what needs to happen right now so you can continue to run strongly and keep going. Is it time to drink? Are you drinking enough? Do you need to eat something or take in some electrolytes? Are you running relaxed? Is your breathing deep and regular? Are you staying focused on the positive? Are you keeping form? Are you monitoring for blisters, sun exposure, chafing, and other things that might need immediate attention?

To make sure you're staying relaxed and not letting yourself tense up, do a quick body scan by starting at the top of your head and relaxing your body section by section moving downward. Feel your facial muscles relaxing, then the muscles in your neck. Move down to the shoulders, your arms, and your chest. Work your way down to your feet. You'll be able to feel the tension releasing from your body section by section. Repeat this exercise from time to time during the run. It gives you a nice positive activity to focus your attention on, and you can usually tell the difference in the ease of running once you're finished.

Breaking the race down into segments, focusing on the here and now, and narrowing your attention to relaxing each part of your body are all ways of keeping your thoughts positive and productive and thus crowding out negative thinking. Another classic technique for keeping negative thoughts at bay and centering your thinking on a positive notion is repeating a mantra.

WORKING YOUR MANTRA

Along with associating the pain and stress of a difficult run with the idea that I am simply experiencing a natural consequence of performing to my potential, I've found using a mantra to be one of the most effective ways of keeping me on track and in a positive frame of mind. The concept of the mantra comes from the Hindu religion. Technically, a mantra is a charm that by its recitation is meant to set up rhythmic waves that are to produce certain results, but for our purposes, I'll define a mantra as just any short, meaningful phrase that you repeat to yourself in order to direct your mind into useful pathways and avoid harmful thoughts.

Mantras have brought me back from the brink of totally crashing and burning in a race or on a long training run, or at least have gotten me out of a deep funk and back to running with purpose and determination on many occasions. Having an effective mantra is like having a safety net. You can always count on it being there when everything else fails. I always go to my mantra when I'm feeling at my worst, but I'll also start repeating my mantra when I feel my mind wandering and I just need to refocus.

Coming up with your own mantra can really be intriguing. What speaks directly to you? What words evoke a very direct response from you? Mantras can come ready-made. Take, for example, Nike's "Just Do It" advertising slogan. This slogan is a monument to directness and brevity. And it has the advantage of being infinitely applicable. It doesn't matter whether you're running up a steep hill, you're in the 19th mile of a marathon, or you're about to jump out of an airplane, it seems to make perfect sense. You "just" need to "do it," or keep doing it.

And somehow the "just" says it all in a way that simply saying "do it" does not. The "just" says never mind about all those really great and logical reasons for why you shouldn't keep going. "Just" acknowledges them, admits that they are there and very difficult to overcome, but then demands that you turn your back on them and "do it" anyway. "*Just* do it!"

But then you may prefer a mantra that comes directly from your own experiences, one that speaks directly and exclusively to you, something that you have imbued with magic. Early on, a very effective mantra came to me when I found that I was always tensing up whenever I started to feel fatigued during a run. So I got into the habit of telling myself that I needed to switch into totally relaxed running mode. So the phrase "total relaxed running" became my mantra. Or I would just repeat to myself "TRR."

At some point, though, the "total relaxed running" phrase wasn't doing the trick. It would remind me to keep relaxed but as the pain or fatigue increased or some unreal level of effort was required to hold on to my pace or hang on for another 10 miles, just relaxing wasn't enough. So I came up with the mantra, "infinite patience, steely determination." Now here was something I could work with. Patience is paramount in running. Think about your mental state when you're trying to hold your pace during the seventh repetition of eight quarter-mile intervals on the track. Or think about miles 20 through 25 in a marathon. It's not that the effort is too great for you or that you physically can't do it; it's just incredibly hard to endure through it, to wait out that hard effort right to the end. You're plenty willing, but you would just like to have it over with. You need patience.

And right along with patience, you need determination. Of course, determination was part of Chlouber's "inexhaustible well of grit and determination" from Leadville, but having that well inside and accessing it are two different things as I had found out firsthand. Making the concept part of my mantra, I reasoned, might just give me a way to tap into that elusive well. Emphasizing the qualities of patience and determination but jacking them up with fancy adjectives also turned out to be a master stroke. Everyone has patience to some degree, but I needed to be reminded that it was going to take *infinite* patience. And likewise, everybody goes into a race or a long run with determination, but when the sledding gets really rough, I was going to need a special kind of determination, *steely* determination.

This mantra did the trick. It seemed applicable in every situation, not just moments when I felt too tense. Whatever problem I was trying to deal with—painful quads, blisters, a bad stomach, or just sheer exhaustion—it was always good to remind myself that I needed to be patient and determined. The more I used it, the more it had the ability to calm me down in any situation, and the more I had success with it, the more powerful and useful it became.

Having a mantra seemed to work so well for me that I would tailor-make different mantras for different situations. I run a lot of ultras in Northern California where the courses are often very hilly. In fact, there are some races where you practically never encounter a significant flat section; you're always either climbing or descending. Such courses suit me just fine as I feel I can relax and let the course dictate my pace. If I'm on a steep hill, I'm walking; if I'm on a downhill, I'm running. Either way, I don't have to think too hard about it; I go with the flow.

But I started to notice that when I did hit a flat section, I would struggle. Suddenly it seemed like I had to work to keep running. The flats would highlight the deep fatigue in my quads, calves, and hamstrings. I felt drained of energy, and even the slightest uptick in pace seemed to require an enormous effort. A mile of flat trail would seem to go on forever. The suffering seemed way out of proportion to the progress I was making. Moreover, once I'd convinced myself that I had this problem with flats, I started anticipating the flat sections, dreading them and knowing they would be tough. When I hit a flat section, I'd flood my mind with all sorts of negative thinking, and then, no big surprise, I'd struggle.

© Rob Mann

The author in the act of staying relentlessly positive

So I did something about it. I came up with a mantra targeted specifically to this problem. The mantra was, "flat is good, flat is fast." Now whenever I come to a flat section in a race, I work that mantra, crowding out the negative thinking with the positive message. It took a while to really accept the message and change how I reacted to flat sections, but eventually it sank in, and I no longer even expect to have a problem when I hit a flat spot. Now I say to myself, *Why in the world would I have a problem? Flat is good, flat is fast!*

HEALTHY, UNINJURED, RESTED, UNAFRAID

Another targeted mantra developed out of a problematic run-up to my attempt at the Bear 100 Mile Endurance Run that begins near Logan in northern Utah and ends at Bear Lake in Idaho. The Bear has a reputation for being one of the more challenging races in the country. Much of the race is at altitude, over difficult trails, and through mountains. So knocking out some big training seemed particularly important for this race. Typically, I follow a fairly elaborate and intensive training plan in the three months or so leading up to any 100-mile race so that I can start the run well prepared and confident. This time around, though, events conspired against me.

As soon as I dialed up my work outs, or maybe because I dialed up my workouts, I felt a strong pull in my hamstring that forced me to back off of any extra running for a couple of weeks. Then, not long after getting over the hamstring and back to full training, I felt a tear in a calf muscle and once again had to rest extensively and bring the running back gingerly so as not to aggravate the calf. I started having some very unhappy encounters with the calendar as I saw the critical weeks before the race slip away. But fate wasn't through with me. About a month out, I caught the flu and didn't recover fully until about a week before the race. It was far too late by then to do any meaningful training, so I had to give serious consideration to withdrawing from the race. What was the point? I wasn't trained; I wasn't ready; and I could foresee the course just chewing me up and spitting me out.

But I really hated giving up on all my plans. I had the plane tickets, the hotel reservations, the car rental, and the weekend away from home all arranged with my family. Plus I was going to miss out on my shot at the Bear. I just couldn't pull the trigger on dropping out, so I told myself I was going to build a new mantra just for the occasion that was going to get me through the run. I wasn't well trained, and I didn't feel ready and confident, so I had to work with whatever strengths I did have.

Hmm...after having been laid so low by the flu, I certainly felt healthy now that I had recovered, so I had that: *healthy*. And having beaten back two separate injuries recently and feeling quite solid now, I could at least show up at the race with no ongoing issues, so I had *uninjured*. With all the bed rest and the forcefully curtailed running schedule, I was definitely not overtrained, so I had *rested*. And finally, I needed to buck up my attitude, forget about the training fiasco, and make something positive happen if I was to succeed, so I simply decided that on race day I was going to be *unafraid*. And that became my mantra: *healthy, uninjured, rested, unafraid*, or *HURU* for short. When I put it all together, it seemed like I had a lot going for me.

Race morning I was already thinking the mantra over and over in the hotel room while putting on my running gear. I thought about it waiting for the start, and I repeated it to myself trudging up the first big climb out of Logan. I forced myself to switch to that positive message every time some doubt entered my mind and started to awaken all the concerns about not having trained well enough. Certainly years of long-distance running had given me a lot of built in stamina that came to the fore during the run, but sticking to the modest but very positive message of my mantra was telling as well. I finished the Bear in good order and surprised myself with a time a good two hours under what I had expected. I also finished *healthy, uninjured*, and *unafraid* though I can't claim that I felt *rested* after running 100 miles.

Staying relentlessly positive when you're out there running seems like the no-brainer of all no-brainers, but the truth is that it usually becomes an issue only when the hurting starts, when the rubber really meets the road. It is easy to imagine that you will be able to stay positive through any punishment, but you will really only know when things are at their worst. So pay attention when you're out there. Try different routines for staying positive and learn to recognize when your mind starts to slip in negative ideas. Own the negative thoughts but then move past them to something positive. You get better and better at it as you practice.

CHAPTER 6

RUNNING
AND MINDFULNESS

In ramping up to run in Leadville in late winter and through all of spring, I had done a boat load of running. There were long training runs on the weekends of five or six hours duration, preparatory ultra races of 50 miles and a 100 kilometers, and hefty lunch-time workouts almost daily. I'd been averaging over 50 miles a week with spikes of up to 100 miles a week during weeks that I raced or did back-to-back long runs.

With all those hours inside my own head, it was hardly a surprise that I should pick up on some of the subtleties of my mental state.

Surprisingly, I rarely had the sense of things being boring. I spent a lot of time exploring new roads and trails, so just taking in all the new sights, sounds, and smells would occupy me. My thoughts ranged here and there. Sometimes I'd lose track of my thinking altogether and wonder what had happened to the last hour, or I'd catch myself registering what was going on in my mind as if I were a visitor at a sports, boat, and travel show, wandering around, looking at all the cool stuff.

It strikes me now—now that I have a better understanding of the practice of mindfulness—that all that running was just naturally leading me into a state of mindfulness. I developed a tendency to focus on just the present moment as I ran along, sometimes picking up on all the things around me or sometimes tuning into my thoughts but with something of a detached view of just what those thoughts were. The running was consuming so that I wouldn't be particularly concerned about issues I had going on in my work life or at home or problems I might be facing in the future. As long as I was running, I was pretty much checked out from worries, and when I finished, I'd have a clear sense of accomplishment, a feeling of an inner peace, and a sense that I was now ready to get on with things and take the world by storm. This mindset that I was experiencing while running and the way I felt after a run seemed suspiciously close to just the mindset and the outcomes typically attributed to mindfulness.

Of course, I'm not the only runner who's made the connection between running and mindfulness. If Mark Twain were alive today, he might say you couldn't swing a dead cat without hitting someone blogging on the Internet about running and mindfulness. Articles and books have been written on the subject. The secret is out.

WHAT IS MINDFULNESS?

Mindfulness is the practice of deliberately focusing attention on the thoughts, sensations, and emotions that one is experiencing at the present moment and accepting them without judgment or evaluation. Kabat-Zinn, the original popularizer of mindfulness, describes ordinary thinking as a "deafening waterfall." According to Kabat-Zinn, in daily life, we get lost in this torrent of thoughts, constantly worrying about what happened in the past or what will happen in the future. We attach emotions and judgments to these thoughts, alternately fleeing from what seems unpleasant and clinging to what seems pleasant. The emotions are often direct and powerful. Our mood can turn on a dime as an idea triggers anger or anxiety, and we go from even-keeled to unsteady or adrift. Moreover, we tend to identify ourselves with our thoughts so that when we lurch from one thought to another and one emotion to another, we feel out of control and anxious. Kabat-Zinn claims we need to step out of this torrent of thinking and become observers of our own thoughts.

The key to mindfulness is to be open and observant about what is happening to you in the present moment. You should stop identifying yourself so much with your thoughts and chasing after them and reacting to them. Rather, you should try to experience the present as a flow of thoughts, sensations, and feelings. Make yourself aware of what you are seeing, hearing, and doing. When thoughts and feelings do arise, treat them with curiosity. You should accept that they exist, but at the same time, you should not be particularly judgmental about them. Keep an open mind about them. Once you've acknowledged a thought or feeling, you should move on to the next sensation or feeling that you are experiencing in the present and stay in the moment.

The benefits claimed for mindfulness are legion and are backed by a significant body of research. Implicit in the practice of mindfulness and the emphasis on the present moment is that you are not obsessing over past events or getting yourself upset over future events. You're wholly involved in the present. Not surprisingly, since you are cultivating a technique for dealing with your thoughts without attaching emotions or worry to them, mindfulness tends to reduces stress. It can be used as a coping strategy for anxiety and depression. Individuals suffering from chronic pain have used mindfulness training to either reduce their levels of pain or find ways to better cope with the stress caused by the pain. Mindfulness is thought to help one focus and concentrate. Learning and memorization skills are boosted by mindfulness training. Mindfulness also promotes a general sense of well-being. On an even deeper level, practitioners see mindfulness as a way to reconcile people with what they see as life's impermanence, to live in harmony with day-to-day struggle, and to feel a deeper connection with life and, by extension, the world in general. Who wouldn't want some of that?

CONNECTIONS TO RUNNING

Mindfulness advocates emphasize that almost any pursuit can be done in a mindful way. You can walk down the street mindfully. You can work at your job mindfully. You can shoot pool mindfully. So of course you can run mindfully. In fact, there are many things about running that seem to invite the practice of mindfulness.

Mindfulness instructors commonly suggest meditating and concentrating on breathing as starting points for their students to enter into a state of mindfulness. Focusing on breathing is a way to empty the mind of other thoughts and feelings and center you on the here and now. Runners have no trouble relating to the process of breathing. For a runner, consciousness of breathing is always either right on or just below the surface. Breathing frames and fuels the act of running.

The rhythmic nature of running is another way running connects with meditation and, by extension, mindfulness. A runner's stride is like a metronome, akin to repeating a mantra when meditating. The swinging of the arms, the motion of the stride, the feet contacting the ground, along with breathing, are all repetitive actions fundamental to running that form a constant background like the beat in music. A runner need only focus on one of these motions to get the same effect as someone meditating gets by focusing on breathing or on a mantra.

By definition, when you go for a run, you are physically separating yourself from your daily workaday world just as if you went into a separate room to meditate and practice mindfulness. Your mind automatically gets a chance to refocus. And along with the physical separation comes a break, to some degree, from the daily mental grind of concerns, worries, plans, ego, social roles, and other distractions that you are usually immersed in. Instead, you are free to pay attention to your immediate experiences—the sensations and sights and sounds of running. In other words, you're free to practice mindfulness.

Running also tends to create the same kind of openness or objectiveness toward your thoughts that one associates with mindfulness. Out on a run, you tend to be outside of your usual social roles, your ego-driven persona. Running down a trail, there can be a reduction in your self-consciousness and your self-criticism. Consequently, you don't bring all that baggage to every thought that comes into your mind. Perhaps this is why a simple solution will often present itself for some vexing problem at work, or a knotty relationship concern will suddenly appear less threatening. Running just seems to create this altered way of processing your thoughts that is very close to the way mindfulness orients thinking.

© Gary Dudney

Mindfulness encourages you to stay in the moment and narrow your focus down to the here and now.

PRACTICING MINDFULNESS

Practicing mindfulness on a run is not complicated, and it's very flexible. You can pretty much turn it on and off whenever you feel like it. Mindfulness can play a role in any running scenario: training, racing, a long run, a short run, as part of an intense workout, or as part of an easy, recovery jog. It draws on Eastern religious practices and philosophy, but mindfulness isn't inherently spiritual or religious. Instead, it relies on a commonsense approach to how the brain works and how people normally think.

While running seems to naturally promote a state of mindfulness, you can certainly deepen the process by consciously and actively working at being mindful as you run. The goal is to get yourself to pay attention to the present moment and cultivate a non-judgmental awareness of the unfolding of your experiences—that is, the sensations, thoughts, and feelings going through your mind.

A good place to start is with all the physical sensations that naturally occur while running. Pay attention to your breathing. Notice the passage of air in and out, the expansion of your lungs, the working of the diaphragm, and the changes when you labor up a hill or when you slow down or when you pick up the pace. Make yourself aware of your feet contacting the ground, the swinging of your arms, the raising of your knees, the whole motion and flow of your running stride. Feel the wind against your skin, and register the heat or the coolness in the air.

Now widen your focus to the world around you—what you're seeing, what you're smelling, and what you're hearing. You don't have to force it by frantically trying to notice absolutely everything around you. Just be aware of what catches your attention. If your route becomes so familiar that you stop noticing things, mix in some new routes that include different scenery or different challenges, such as hills or a rough trail. By concentrating on your physical sensations and what is going on around you as you run along, you are practicing keeping your focus on the present moment and, of course, off the past and future and the worries and concerns associated with them.

Invariably, thoughts will arise in your mind of work issues or of a concern about some future event that will tug you away from your focus on the present. Your task is to acknowledge the thought and any feelings and emotions associated with the thought, but then gently direct your attention back to your run and the present moment. With practice, it will become easier and easier to simply register thoughts going through your mind as simply part of the flow of ideas, sensations, and feelings that make up the present moment. You do not need to attach yourself to these thoughts, be overwhelmed by them, or even think of your thoughts as making up what is you. Freed from oppressive thoughts and able to simply run along and exist in the moment, you experience your run as even more liberating, stress reducing, and rewarding than ever before.

USING MINDFULNESS

Even if you're not attempting to make mindfulness a constant as you run, you can still profitably use different mindfulness techniques in certain situations. As anyone who has completed a marathon or run their hardest to set a PR in a 10K or even suffered through just one interval workout on a track knows, running can involve a lot of pain. Top performances don't happen without moving out of your comfort zone. Fortunately, one of the proven benefits of practicing mindfulness is having a way to deal with pain. One of Kabat-Zinn's original studies that brought so much attention to mindfulness involved helping patients deal with chronic pain.

Typically, when discomfort begins in a run, you try to resist it, get rid of it, suppress it, ignore it, or somehow fight it off. Of course, none of that works. The pain just grows in your mind accompanied with anxiety about your ability to keep going. Mindfulness counsels that you should take just the opposite approach to pain. When you start experiencing pain, you should move toward the pain, embrace it, fully acknowledge it, and even sink down into the feeling and experience it as directly as possible. Once you quit resisting and instead embrace the pain, it loses some of its power over you. You experience it more as just another feeling, another sensation. It is part of being in the moment. After acceptance can come dismissal. You can direct your focus toward other things you are experiencing and let the pain recede into the background.

Of course, by pain we are talking about the sensations you normally experience as a result of sustained activity, a feeling of general discomfort, pain that disappears once the activity stops. If you start experiencing a sharp, localized pain that could signal an injury, you need to back off running and not try to push through the pain. Take a day or two off of running to see what happens. If the issue persists, get professional help.

Besides pain management, mindfulness can be used to cope with the other discomforts of running. If you feel fatigued, don't try to convince yourself that somehow you're not fatigued. Acknowledge the feeling, sink down into it, recognize it as part of the process of running hard for a long time, and then gently move your thoughts on to the next sensation. Eventually you'll learn to recognize that these feelings of discomfort are not show stoppers, but rather just sensations that you can cope with without fear or anxiety becoming part of the process.

The mindfulness process of coping with pain and other discomfort is somewhat similar to Dahlkoetter's process described before of replacing negative thoughts with positive ones. Dahlkoetter would have you acknowledge the pain and then see it in a positive light as evidence of you achieving your goals. With mindfulness, the process and technique are similar, but the emphasis is more on taking an objective attitude toward the pain, examining it, experiencing it for what it is, seeing it as one of many sensations that are present in the moment, but not attaching any particular emotions to it.

A TALE OF TWO HUNDREDS

Practicing mindfulness while I ran deepened the enjoyment I got out of my daily workouts and seemed to even heighten the sense of accomplishment and inner peace I felt after each run. During long runs or intense workouts such as interval training, I found I could cope with the painful aspects of the process better and moderate or eliminate the stress I used to feel about pushing myself way out of my comfort zone.

When I looked back at some of my peak experiences as a runner, I could clearly see how practicing mindfulness had changed my approach to running and how some failures in the past might have played out very differently had I employed a different mindset at the time. One stark example for me was a DNF I had suffered at the Western States Endurance Run early in my attempts at mastering 100-mile races. Back then I would line up to start a 100-miler and really have no idea how it was going to go or whether I would finish. It was a crap shoot. A host of physical or mental issues against which I had no effective defenses seemed ready to jump up and stop me. Nowadays, being well fortified with mindfulness training, I line up and feel virtually certain that I will finish.

Ironically, my troubles the year of my DNF at Western States began after I had already made it through the hottest, most challenging section of the course—the deep canyons where the temperatures typically get over 100 degrees Fahrenheit, the trail is rugged, and the climbs are legendary. I'd endured the elevation in the high country, the notoriously steep climb at Devil's Thumb, and the huge climb out of El Dorado Canyon that leads to the aid station at Michigan Bluff. I had just one relatively small canyon to cross, Volcano Canyon, and I would be at Foresthill, mile 62, and the gateway to the rest of the course, which is generally considered much easier than the part I'd already covered. It seemed like I was on the verge of mission accomplished.

But as I turned onto the single track that would take me down into Volcano Canyon, I started registering the soreness in my legs, the drowsiness I felt as I headed into the evening, and the sheer fatigue of running for so long. I'd been at it since five in the morning. I also had some blisters bothering me, and my stomach didn't feel particularly great. Suddenly I had this very strong impulse to escape all this discomfort by quitting.

The idea latched on to my mind like a leech and quickly sucked me into a downward spiral of negative thinking. Of course, paramount was this notion that if I felt bad, then how was I going to feel later on in the night, later on *all* night? My finish wouldn't be until late in the morning, a time that seemed so unreasonably far off that it bordered on impossible. The idea that things could only get worse and worse filled me with dread. My legs would get unbearably sore; the drowsiness would slow me to a crawl just extending the suffering; the nausea would get worse until I threw up; and blisters would form on top of the blisters I already had and plague me with each step.

On top of obsessing over what was to come, I conjured up all my past failures and brought the full weight of that baggage down on myself as well. I failed those times. Why should I think I wouldn't fail now? I lost touch with the here and now altogether as I dwelt on all the difficulties I knew were coming and the failures of the past. I was anything but dispassionate about analyzing my situation. Every thought was freighted with dread and fear. My anxiety soared unchecked.

I made my decision. It wasn't my day, I told myself. Look how many problems are stopping me. Look how horrible the rest of the race is going to be. I was done. If I quit, I wouldn't have to struggle to reach the next aid station and the next, and I wouldn't have to face the awful, long night. It will all be over. I was comfortable with my decision. That was that. I quit.

I walked a good deal of the rest of the way through the canyon. Having quit, I was immediately much more relaxed. By the time I got up to the road that led to Foresthill, I was ready for a little jog to hurry up and get it over with. I trotted into Foresthill feeling very serene. "I'm quitting," I said to Robert Josephs, my friend who happened to be there crewing for me that year.

He was shocked. He looked at me like I'd just pulled a skunk out of my waist belt. "You're ahead of schedule," he blurted. "You look great. You're moving fine."

"Nope. I'm done," I said. "It was just too much." I was adamant.

Robert swore I would end up hating myself, but nothing he said was going to make any difference to me. Getting out of the race was all I cared about. Of course, two days later, I hated myself.

Back in Volcano Canyon, I had made some classic mistakes from the perspective of mindfulness. When the idea of quitting arose, I had attached myself to it whole hog and owned it. I let it quickly drag me out of the present and into thinking about all sorts of past and future problems—both real and imagined.

I completely lost contact with my ongoing sensations and the world around me. Had I stayed in the moment and focused without judgment or emotion on the actual sensations I was experiencing, I might have recognized that I was having problems, yes, but they weren't actually that severe and were even quite manageable. I might have tried a little walking to give my legs a break and taken some acetaminophen for the aching. A little ginger or some added electrolytes might have helped settle my stomach. A cup of coffee at the next aid station probably would have taken care of the drowsiness. A few easy fixes, then, and I might have really felt quite human. Even if none of the remedies had worked, I still could have persisted, accepting each issue as just another sensation passing through my consciousness along with a lot of other sensations and thoughts.

Moreover, the sun had set. The punishing heat of the day was over. The air was getting cooler. The Sierra Nevada landscape all around me was beautiful. The trail was in good shape, and the way down into Volcano Canyon was an easy, gentle slope. All in all, for being in the 60th mile of a 100-mile run, my situation was quite good. If I had only gently pushed that idea about quitting aside and not attached myself to it and then allowed myself to really experience what was happening to me and remained in the moment, I think that race would have had a much different outcome.

A few years later, I was at a similar stage of a 100-mile race, although a little bit later in the night. It was the San Diego 100 held in the mountainous region of Southern California east of San Diego. It wasn't as difficult a race course as Western States, but it was still hilly and full of challenges—some big climbs and lots of rough, rocky trail. I was running down a jeep road that dropped into a valley. A full moon drenched the forest around me in a milky light and made my headlamp unnecessary. There was a wide stream running down the slope next to the road. The rushing water chattered softly next to me. The moonlight sparkled off the rifts and ridges in the water. The woods were dead quiet and still. The masses of pine limbs crisscrossing above the forest floor were as motionless as if the forest were a painting.

I was all alone and running along practically in a trance. The sensation of my feet hitting the road, the motion of my arms and legs with each stride, my breathing, the cool air, the stream and moonlight, and the silent trees were the only things I was aware of. Now keep in mind that I was 70 miles into a tough trail race. I'd been running at that point for about 20 hours. I had another eight hours to go, and the aid stations behind me were littered with prostrate runners who had wilted under the strain of the heat, the distance, the rugged trail, and the sheer burden of eating and drinking enough to fuel a body through such a regimen without bonking, throwing up, or succumbing to some other imbalance in fuel, electrolytes, fluids, guts, or determination.

But this time, I wasn't thinking of the tough miles behind me or the struggle ahead of me. I was perfectly and completely in the moment, feeling the sensations of my body moving through space and taking in the night sky above me and the forest around me. I was running mindfully. I noticed some aches and pains, sure, and I was tired, but when these things led to thoughts of quitting, I was easily able to acknowledge the thoughts, push them aside, and return to the moment. The main impression I had as I ran along was an overwhelming sense of peacefulness and well-being. I was happy as could be. I finished that race later in the morning with no problem.

© Gary Dudney

When you run mindfully, you fully experience the beauty of the land, you hear the crunch of gravel under your feet, and you feel the warmth of the air on your skin.

OTHER REWARDS

So just on a practical level, it's apparent how useful mindfulness can be when applied to running in coping with painful sensations, turning negative thoughts aside, enhancing the stress relief benefits of running, and enriching the experience of running in general. But mindfulness offers additional, perhaps more profound, rewards that can be sought while you're running or by practicing mindfulness during other activities of your life.

Mindfulness practitioners claim that mindfulness promotes a sense of connection to the world around you. The explanation goes something like this: As you learn to avoid thinking of your thoughts and feelings as being your "self," and instead perceive of the whole flow of sensations, emotions, and ideas passing through your mind as more who you are, your sense of self starts to diminish and eventually disappear. So where you normally think of the world as being comprised of your "self" and everything else being "other," with the disappearance of self, you lose that separation between you and the other—that is, the rest of the world. With the barrier gone, you feel more directly connected to things as if you and all the other creatures and things around are all of a piece.

Just as mindfulness can serve to break down the barriers between you and the rest of the world, it breaks down the barriers between you and other people. Since you are living in the moment and avoiding the entrapments of your usual ego-driven persona, you are more open to others and more empathetic. You are also less judgmental and free to connect with others' experiences and sufferings.

Finally, mindfulness promotes a general sense of well-being and equanimity. Mark Twain said, "I am an old man and have known a great many troubles, but most of them never happened." Freed from the constant anxiety caused by dwelling on bad things that might happen in the future and able to accept and move beyond things that happened in the past, you naturally have a better feeling about just living in the present. You are less susceptible to being swept away by negative, impulsive emotions. You are accepting of the way things are and the fact that change in life is natural and constant.

CHAPTER 7

GRAND SLAMMED

"What are you doing in here?"

The voice was angry, accusatory, and disgusted. Kathy Welch stood in the doorway of the medical tent where I was stretched out on a cot under a sleeping bag. She was a long-time friend. I'd shared many races with her and chatted away miles of trail in the process. She was unfailingly friendly, kind, upbeat, and positive. Right now, she looked pissed off as hell.

"I'm quitting," I said.

A grin replaced her scowl, and she laughed. "No, you're not. You can't quit. You're in the Grand Slam."

And that was true. I was back trying to finish the Leadville 100, at which I had failed so miserably the year before. This year, however, I had set my sights even higher. I was attempting the Grand Slam of Ultrarunning: a series of four designated 100-mile races that must be done in a single summer with minimal recovery time between races. Besides Leadville, the other races of the Grand Slam are Western States, the Vermont 100, and the Wasatch Front 100 in Utah near Salt Lake City. So you not only had to do all the races, but you had to travel all over the country to get to them.

When Kathy found me in the tent, I had already made it through Western States and Vermont, and I had just 25 miles to go to finish Leadville. All that was left was Wasatch, and I'd be lifting a magnificent Grand Slam finisher's eagle trophy over my head. But instead, I was quitting.

"My ankles are killing me," I gasped. "I messed them up in Vermont. I thought they were better."

"Get up, and let's go," Kathy said.

"I can't."

"I'll park my car a mile down the road," she said, "where you get off the blacktop and start up Sugarloaf. Just walk to my car, and we'll talk."

I groaned. Images of Chlouber telling the crowd that the one thing we could not do is quit flashed through my head. "Make pain your friend," he'd said. Well, I'd managed to do that in spades. I'd spent hours trying to stay positive, accept the pain, and move past it. I'd worked the hell out of all my mantras and tried every other trick in the book, but having a swelling, urgent pain well up from each ankle on every step had just been too much. I had slowed to a crawl by the time I'd gotten back to the Fish Hatchery aid station and the medical staff there had said they could not provide any painkillers. They'd offered me a cot instead, and I'd taken it.

But now Kathy had me. The pain screaming out of my ankles made it impossible to face the 10-mile stretch to May Queen, but a mile to a car that could give me a ride home if I wanted, that I could maybe handle. Plus, being off my feet for a while had helped.

I pushed off the cot. Kathy had my waist belt back around me before I knew what she was doing. She ran off to fill my water bottles. She did everything but kick me in the butt as I limped back out onto the course and onto the road toward Sugarloaf.

The Colorado night was still and quiet. The air in the Rocky Mountains was crisp. There were no cars, no other runners. It was just me on the blacktop road following the dim light from my headlamp, pine trees forming a dark wall on either side. Every step hurt; the shooting pain from my ankles stayed urgent and intense. There was no lessening into a bearable ache, just sheer agony. I didn't know what I'd done to my ankles, but the level of pain seemed to suggest something serious.

I saw Kathy's car in the distance and her standing next to it. Despite the pain, I seemed to be able to keep moving forward. If I could just get to May Queen and then on to the finish, maybe I could recover in time for Wasatch. There was still hope. I reached Kathy, gave her a hug, and said, "If anything good comes out of this, I have you to thank."

"Hang tough, Gary," she said. "It's the Grand Slam."

I stepped off the road onto a short stretch of trail that followed the edge of the forest. Where the trail turned into the trees and up the steep climb over Sugarloaf Pass, I stopped. I had finished the little jog over to Kathy's car on the flat road, the easy part. Now I was facing a big ascent and the rest of the trip to May Queen—the last aid station before the finish. Time was running short, and my ankles were on fire again, murdering me with each step. I looked up at the trail and thought, *Goddam you, Robert Josephs, this is all your fault!*

THE RUN-UP

Robert Josephs was my running buddy who had talked me into trying the Grand Slam against my better judgment. He and I were not the first runners who would come to mind when you thought about the Grand Slam. Both of us had been to Leadville once before and failed. While I had managed to get halfway in my attempt, Robert hadn't even gotten that far.

On my first attempt at Western States, I'd quit at Foresthill, mile 62. On my second attempt, I'd finished but with only 23 minutes to spare before the final cutoff of 30 hours. Robert had racked up three finishes at Western States, but had also come up short four other times. Neither of us had even tried Wasatch, which many runners claim is the hardest of the four races. So the two of us successfully completing all four races back to back in one summer seemed like a very remote proposition.

When Robert first raised the possibility that we should sign up for the Slam, I told him, "Wild horses could not drag me back to Leadville this year." I was determined to get back there eventually and get my hug from Merilee O'Neil, but the sting was still there from my first try, and I was convinced that to have any chance of finishing, I needed at least two solid years of focused training and maybe several trips to the top of Mt. Everest before I would be ready.

But if Robert was anything, he was persistent and stubborn, traits he had parlayed into becoming a runner despite a childhood bout with polio that had left him with a limping, awkward gait. Medium build, medium height, but strong and solid as an ox, he had been raised in a large Jewish family in Philadelphia. With his olive skin and brown hair and eyes, he wouldn't have looked out of place walking the streets of Tel Aviv, except he'd be limping.

Robert was not one to suffer fools easily, which is why he met much of the blather I constantly spouted when we were out training together with dead silence. When he did speak, it was usually direct and to the point. He was amused by my habit of over drinking early in a run and then having to pee behind every bush along the trail until I got back into equilibrium. He told me I was the hero of dogs everywhere. Sitting on a plane once, waiting to take off, I showed him an ad for some *Lord of the Rings* trinkets. "Hey," I said, "you should get some of this *Lord of the Rings* stuff."

"Yeah, Lord of the Rinky-Dink," he shot back without hesitation.

Way back in 1980, when the very first American River 50 Mile Endurance Run was being held in Sacramento, Robert was at the starting line. It was a time when finishing a marathon was still considered a supreme running achievement. Running 50 miles wasn't even part of the known universe. Since then, he'd run American River 23 times, putting him fourth on the all-time list of most finishes at that event. Robert had a great running past, but he wanted the Grand Slam.

"We're getting old," he argued. (He was 46 at the time; I was 50.)

"We're never going to be in better shape than we are right now. We're going to get more injured as time goes by, not less. I'm going to do it, so we might as well do it together and split the costs. You'll never, ever have a better chance."

I guess I was swayed by the part about splitting the costs.

After we signed up for the four races, we were out on a trail somewhere training, and Robert very casually mentioned, "I signed up for the Last Great Race."

"What?!" I exclaimed. The Last Great Race was the Grand Slam plus two additional races, still done all in one summer, and the two extra races were tough ones. I figured the odds of us finishing the Slam were about one in a thousand. Finishing the Last Great Race? No way. "Why would you do that?" I asked.

"Because anyone can do the Grand Slam," Robert replied.

Now that we were committed, the next step was dealing with all the mechanics and logistics. Planning for the summer was like Napoleon's preparation for the invasion of Russia, except Napoleon didn't have two teenage kids and a full-time job. Reservations for planes, hotel rooms, and rental cars had to be made. There were volunteer requirements to fulfill. There was recruiting pacers and crew, finding people who could travel to Colorado, Vermont, and Utah. I ordered more shoes, bought more drop bags, and stocked up on energy gel. I leafed through catalogues for the latest in high-tech flashlights and lightweight shells. I spent every weekend running punishing long workouts on gnarly trails. I entered a whole series of springtime races. I set aside Memorial Day weekend for the Western States training camp.

Inevitably, the training we did seemed inadequate. Even the most elaborate training runs, six hours of humping up and down the hillsides around Monterey, would pale in comparison to what we knew we would face at Western States in the high country or the climbs at Wasatch. Plus, the Monterey Bay area where we both lived never got hot enough for heat training and was obviously too low for altitude training. How in the world could we be ready for the machine gunning we would endure over the summer?

All in all it was a very anxious spring. Time crept by so slowly I swore I was looking at the same Panda bear on my wildlife calendar for three or four months before I finally got to flip it over to the stolid-looking Galapagos turtles. I obsessed over every little ache and pain, certain my sore hamstring was going to turn into a career-ending injury or that the pain in the arch of my foot was a stress fracture. I imagined myself walking around in a cast while Robert was leaping happily over Hope Pass at Leadville.

And then, without warning, it was June. The Grand Slam race dates for 2003 were Western States, June 28; Vermont, July 19; Leadville Trail, August 16; and Wasatch Front, September 6. Western States created some kind of weird time-warp vortex that sucked up all of June. The race was three weeks off one day, I took a sip of coffee, and the race was that weekend.

WESTERN STATES

Western States is the very spot where Gordon Ainsleigh touched off 100-mile trail racing in America when he famously decided he could run the 100 miles of trail that the horses normally traversed for the Tevis Cup Western States Trail Ride. His success at finishing the horse race course on foot in 1974 is what led to the Western States 100 Mile Endurance Run. And amazingly, when we got to Squaw Valley where the race begins, the very same Gordon Ainsleigh was right there, walking around at the orientation, laughing with his friends, still running the race himself and perhaps looking to do it under 24 hours, which earns the runner a special silver belt buckle. It was like visiting Appomattox Courthouse and finding Grant and Lee still sitting at the table, shooting the breeze.

"The hardest 50-mile race I ever ran was the first 50 miles at Western States," one of my running buddies had told me. Waiting for the start on Saturday morning, it struck me that four out of every ten runners around me were not going to cross the finish line at Placer High in Auburn. I wondered which group I would be in. Then the moment arrived, and the long months of anticipation were suddenly over. Robert and I wished each other well, and the clock ticked down to zero. The race and the Grand Slam were on.

I was nervous striding up the big, initial climb to Emigrant Pass. Was it hard to breathe at this altitude, or was I just tense? Was I exhausting myself, starting out too hard? Who was ahead of me? Who was behind me? I took some deep breaths to relax. I started to notice that people around me were comparing notes on the Grand Slam.

A typical conversation went: "First time at Western?"

"No, I've done it before."

"Doin' Vermont?"

"Yeah."

"You slammin'?"

"Yeah. You, too?"

"Yeah."

There seemed to be a certain calculated lack of enthusiasm in how people owned up to being Grand Slammers, like they were scared they might jinx the whole thing by being too direct about it so early in the game.

Topping the rise at Emigrant Pass, I turned to look at the long sweep of Squaw Valley, far below me now, and Lake Tahoe in the distance. The dawn had come and with it a strange feeling. I felt like I was leaving something behind. There was my life before I attempted the Grand Slam. That was over. Whatever I would experience from here on out would be in the context of having tried this massive thing.

Skipping down the curving sweep of single track on the far side of the pass, I had my first premonition that things would go well for me. The climb had not fazed me. I was running comfortably and easily keeping up with the runners around me. The long transition through the Granite Chief Wilderness along the ridge flowed by despite the many rocks, the tricky footing, the roller-coaster jigs and jags of the trail, and the slippery stream crossings. In my past two attempts at Western, I had arrived at Robinson Flat, the first major aid station at about mile 30, feeling beat up and worn out. This year I felt fine.

So I headed into the next segment of the course, the dreaded deep canyons, miles 30 through 60, feeling pretty spiffy. But then it got hot, and I mean hot—over 100 degrees hot. I started dunking my head in every stream, bucket, sponge, horse trough, and mud hole I could find. At the bottom of Deadwood Canyon, just before the storied Devil's Thumb climb, I made a bee line for the river that would have astonished bees. It looked like a beach party along the shore. Runners were stretched out on the rocks with their feet in the water. Some were actually sitting in the river and submerging themselves completely. I got on my knees and used my hat to pour water over my head. The icy water felt like shock therapy.

When I felt cooled down, I started the trip up the tight switchbacks of Devil's Thumb. As hot and torturous as it was, this climb actually worked out well for me. I was passing runners who were stopped, bent over, hands on knees, succumbing to the heat. One guy threw up as I went by, yet I was able to keep up a steady march to the top. Slowly but surely, the hot canyons passed by under my slow but relentless assault. The afternoon passed, and I eased into Foresthill, mile 62, where on my first try at Western I had thrown in the towel.

At Foresthill, I picked up my pacer, and we headed out of town and down into the canyon above the Middle Fork of the American River. I seemed to get into a zone that included my mind being occupied by a constant stream of Doors songs. I didn't seem to have any control over the song selection or the volume. My mind was just on autopilot. "Come on, Baby, light my fire, try to set the night on fire…" "People are strange when you're a stranger…" "I'm a backdoor man…" "This is the end, my one true friend, the end…" The music in my head was so loud I thought my pacer could hear it. The aid stations kept appearing out of the dark like cheap bars on ruined streets and then disappearing behind us like jilted lovers. The air was cool now. We got down beside the river, and I could hear the water rushing by next to me.

The river crossing at Rucky Chucky looked like a scene out of *Apocalypse Now*, weird jerky lighting and people stumbling around like zombies. I actually enjoyed the whole diverting process of crossing the river and sitting on the far side, changing clothes and wolfing down food. It broke up the continuous running. Along the Auburn Lakes Trail section of the course that came next, I managed to fight off sleep and exhaustion so that by the time I'd reached Brown's Bar at 90 miles, I knew I was home free. All my exhaustion fell away as the light came up, and I approached the Highway 49 crossing just seven miles from the finish. I floated over the final trails, stunned that it was possible to feel so good at the end of a 100-mile run.

Reaching the Placer High School stadium in Auburn, I sped around the track and finished in 27 hours, 13 minutes. That was well over an hour faster than the goal I had set for myself and almost two and a half hours better than my previous finish at Western. It was a great moment, but then it suddenly took a wrong turn. My wife was there, and after things quieted down, she said, "Robert didn't make it."

I was stunned. We'd hopscotched with each other at the beginning of the race, but then I had gotten slightly ahead. That kept us separated all the way to Michigan Bluff at 55 miles, but I'd seen him there coming in just as I was leaving. He was still just a few minutes behind at Foresthill. At Highway 49, I'd heard that he had taken quite a bit of extra time to get to the river crossing, but that he was across and pushing on. I learned later that things had gone downhill from there. A bad stomach touched off by the heat had kept him from eating enough. The lack of energy caught up with him later in the night. At the Auburn Lake Trails station, he calculated that at the pace he was going he was not going to make the cutoff at the finish, so he dropped there. I'd lost my partner in crime.

Crossing the river at Rucky Chucky at Western States.

We traveled home separately, and I didn't hear from Robert for three days. Then he sent an email. He was sorry that he wasn't going to be able to help me through the rest of the Grand Slam, because, he wrote, "I'll be running the races myself and trying to beat you to the finish." So he was going to continue with the other three races even though he'd lost his chance at the Grand Slam. I wondered how I would have reacted in his place. Chances are I would have moped around and then sandbagged the other races. Not Robert.

VERMONT

It's hard to describe just how strange it seemed arriving in Vermont from California. The Central Coast around Monterey, California, is all green hills and wildflowers in the early spring, but in the summer, the place reverts back to its semi-desert, low-rainfall character. The plant life goes to seed and dies. The hills turn brown. Riparian lakes and ponds dry up, and the earth cracks. As we arrived in Vermont, from the plane it looked as if we were arriving in the Amazon. Everything was green. Everything was growing. The fields were lush expanses of thick grass. The trees were covered in broad, healthy leaves.

The two races, Western States and Vermont, are also a study in contrast. The Western States trail passes through rugged mountains and isolated canyons. Signs of civilization are few and far between. In Vermont, the foothills of the Green Mountains are low and rolling. Farms are scattered along the country roads. Cabins pop out of the woods at every turn. Stone walls line the roads. Western passes through the crumbling remains of the Gold Rush era—abandoned graveyards deep in the forest, rusting mining equipment. In Vermont, the stone churches, covered bridges, village greens, and Federal-style houses evoke early America and the colonial past. Western is gold miners and lumberjacks. Vermont is dairy farmers and innkeepers.

Robert and I sat in our hotel room in Woodstock, fiddling with the alarm clock and working out when we needed to get up. The race start was at four in the morning. It was going to take us about an hour to get up and get ready. We left another half an hour for the drive over in case we got lost, which, as a matter of fact, we did. We set the alarm for two o'clock Eastern time, which was 11 o'clock Pacific time, our time. Neither of us slept a wink.

The race began to the strains of "Chariots of Fire" played on an electric piano with bursts of fireworks going off overhead. But the excitement quickly dissipated as we entered a dark forest and picked our way over a muddy trail with our flashlights. In the close, foggy air, my breathing echoed in my head. The first trails gave way to country roads lined with crumbling stone walls and maple forests. Fog hung low over duck ponds next to the road where cattails hugged the shore, and frogs croaked dissolutely. I monitored the state of my legs and wondered if exhaustion from the lack of sleep and the second 100-mile effort was going to come crashing down on me early in the race, but all was normal.

Because of the early start, it seemed like we had been running forever by the time early afternoon rolled around. The weather had been very forgiving. Prepared for heat and humidity, I kept looking up at a broken cloud cover that was keeping the sun in check. We were catching a real break here. Compared to Western, this was like running in the Arctic.

At the 60-mile mark of the race, I took stock. Nothing major was going wrong. I was handling the second hundred in good order. It was looking like a definite finish in Vermont, but more importantly, for the very first time since agreeing to the Grand Slam, I was feeling like I might actually have a shot at going all the way. I had been careful to keep that kind of optimism in check for fear of feeding too much red meat to the monster of disappointment that might be waiting around the next corner. But now hope came spewing out of me like fizz from a dropped soda can.

Around 90 miles, we climbed a road up the aptly named Blood Hill. Along the climb, glow sticks beckoned from high above like distant stars. The final miles snaked along a hillside through the woods, the trail constantly shifting up and down. I had developed pains at the top of both feet just where the foot meets the ankle. I attributed it to the pounding my feet had taken throughout the day on some unforgiving hard road surfaces that were prevalent on the course in Vermont. A similar thing had happened to me the year before in Kansas in a race that was also run extensively on hard, dry country roads and rock-hard trails. But a little ankle pain wasn't going to dampen my soaring spirits. I was just a few miles from the end of the race, and I had only been running for 22 hours. It looked like I would be collecting a silver belt buckle reserved for those who finished in less than 24 hours.

I trotted up to the finish line in front of a big horse barn. No one seemed to notice me as a local favorite had just finished ahead of me and was drawing everyone's attention. I walked into the barn and sat down in the first folding chair I came to. Someone, a stranger, draped a big horse blanket over my shoulders. It was just after four in the morning, and the air had that damp intense chill that comes just before dawn. I could hardly believe I had just made it through Vermont. Half of the Grand Slam was done.

Robert found me a couple of hours later fast asleep in the back of our rental car. He told me he'd dropped out with just ten miles to go. I was too wiped out to realize that he was kidding. He strung me along for a while and then told me the truth. Actually, he'd finished in 25:40. It was a new 100-mile personal best for him, so we'd both come through Vermont smelling like roses.

LEADVILLE REWIND

A little over four weeks later, I found myself back in the shabby Sixth Street Gym in Leadville, Colorado, waiting for Chlouber's infamous pep talk. Bill Finkbeiner was up at the front of the room, showing his son the specially made belt buckle that he was expected to take home for finishing Leadville for the twentieth consecutive time. It was as big as a dinner plate. The race was 21 years old at that point. Finkbeiner had been invited to the first running of the race, but he had declined.

Chlouber interrupted his usual remarks to introduce someone in the crowd. "Now here's a feller who has raised the bar on toughness," Chlouber said. "Yessir, this gentleman is just plain old Leadville rock hard, horse leather tough." Then he asked Aron Ralston to stand up. It was the very individual who a couple of months before had been pinned to a rock wall by a boulder and had had to cut his own arm off to save his life. This was long before the book and the James Franco movie had come out, but everyone in the gym had heard the story. Aron was young and handsome. He stood up, smiled, and waved genially. A new prosthetic arm was strapped to his shoulder. The plan was for him to pace this year and then run the race himself the following year. When the standing ovation finally quieted down, Chlouber said, "So when you get out there in the middle of the night, and you start whinin'…"

At just before five the next morning, Robert and I were standing with 500 other runners on the corner of Sixth and Harrison. I pulled out my gloves and put them on. I strapped the safety loop of my flashlight around my wrist. With five minutes to go, I worked my way up closer to the start banner. I was not calm, but then I wasn't scared either. This was our third start this summer. I was very aware that patience was required. Nothing big would happen for the next 10 or 12 hours. Then we'd engage the beast.

A shotgun blast sent us down Sixth Street, and I immediately lost track of Robert in the mad rush to get out of town. I spent some time adjusting my stride and settling down on the Boulevard heading toward Turquoise Lake. Once we made the single track next to the lake, I was running comfortably and even moving up on runners who had gone out too fast and were having to cut their speed back. The only surprise was that I was getting a mild little pain in the front of both my ankles. I recognized the pain as an echo of the problem I'd had during the last 10 miles of Vermont. Both ankles had gotten quite painful then, but the problem cleared up in no time after the race and hadn't bothered me in any of the running I'd done in the past four weeks before Leadville. I'd forgotten all about it. *Okay*, I thought, *I'm going to have this minor irritant going on. Big deal. Pain's my friend. Grit and determination. Think of Aron Ralston for God's sake!* I started my ibuprofen regimen a bit sooner than I'd planned and put it out of my mind.

We reached May Queen after two and a half hours, and I was relieved to see I was right on my planned schedule. I scarfed down some food, filled my water bottles, and set out over the Colorado Trail for Sugarloaf Pass. I remembered struggling up this road toward the pass last year. This year, I pushed through the same section with short walks and long runs and figured I was putting some time in the bank for later. At the Fish Hatchery, I was actually ahead of schedule! *Can this really be happening?* I asked myself.

The next section of the course from the Fish Hatchery around to Halfmoon was deceptive. Still early in the race, it seemed like a flat, paved road curving along the floor of a valley at the lowest altitude of the race would be a breeze. But we were still well over 9,000 feet, and the altitude was getting to me, as it did to most people who had the temerity to live at sea level and not spend three weeks in Leadville ahead of the race. I decided it was time to work some positive thinking

© Gary Dudney

Stream crossings abound in the Rocky Mountains.

magic, so I picked a runner who was going at a slow but steady pace, tucked in behind him, and imagined I was drawing energy from him. It worked. Instead of perhaps slipping off my plan, I made Halfmoon still ahead of schedule and marched right on to the roller-coaster trail to Twin Lakes.

After Twin Lakes was the momentous climb to Hope Pass. I fell in with a group making a steady ascent at a pace that suited me. A sudden rainstorm brought everyone to a halt as we struggled into our rain gear. As we got higher, some disconcerting bolts of lightning crashed around us closer than I would have preferred, but the thought of being struck by lightning did have the useful effect of emptying my mind of all concerns about my sore and tired legs. The year before, this same climb had broken me. This year, it served to confirm that I had the race well in hand.

At Winfield—the halfway point—my elapsed time was only a little over 12 hours. This was massively better than what I had managed the year before. It meant that I had more than 17 hours to get back to the finish. It was a miracle. I could crawl back in that amount of time. I couldn't believe it. *I could kiss Robert Josephs right now*, I thought. *What a great and fabulous idea it was to tackle the Grand Slam this year!* Next stop, Wasatch, and then I'll be lifting that big eagle trophy over my head to deafening applause.

CHAPTER 8

UNLEASHING YOUR INNER TRAIL MONSTER

There is another approach to running, perhaps not as introspective as cultivating mindfulness, but still a very rewarding and dynamic way to think about your running. It is discovering and developing the trail monster that is locked inside of you.

We marvel at the adaptations that allow cheetahs, for example, to run down prey at 50 miles an hour. We admire the prehensile trunk of the elephant, the baleen grill of an enormous whale that allows it to feed on microscopic plankton, or the giraffe's amazing neck. But we should be equally impressed by our own adaptations that make us exceptional long-distance runners: our upright stance, our stunningly unique feet, and our over-the-top gluteus maximus muscles, the strongest muscle in the human body. Every day, we wake up to these gifts that are the product of about four million years of natural selection, yet in the modern world, for so many, our ability to run, this special natural capacity that we have, is ignored and left wholly undeveloped.

Running, as we've noted before, puts us in touch with our long prehistoric past and activates our physical selves in just the way that humans have been activated since we ventured out of the jungle and ran down our first ungulate. No wonder running can give us such a sense of power and satisfaction. It would be surprising if we didn't feel that way when we tap into this fundamental adaptation of our species.

And there is no better place to develop as a runner than on trails, as so many runners are discovering these days. Participation in trail running is sky rocketing, and trail races are proliferating like rabbits in an out year for the coyote population. But why trails? Isn't running down a road just as good, simpler, and easier to manage? Yes, precisely. That is *why* you want trails! Because you don't want easy and simple...you want tough and complicated. You want the workout that will awaken your inner trail monster.

THE CASE FOR TRAIL RUNNING

Running on a road—a flat, even, and hard surface—you use exactly the same muscles in the same way through the same range of motion and with about the same intensity over and over and over. A hilly route is going to change up the intensity somewhat and shift the load on the muscles to some extent, but the repetitive motion will not be altered significantly. You'll develop the muscles engaged in this motion very well, and you'll get a nice, even cardiovascular, workout. But you'll also be developing yourself into a one-trick pony. I'd put a trail monster up against a one-trick pony any day.

On a trail, the unchanging repetitive motion is gone. The uneven camber of the trail; the obstacles such as rocks, roots, and ruts; and the greater variations in gradient you'll find on a trail will be constantly breaking up your stride and producing a much different workout. The stabilizing muscles in your legs and torso will be constantly adjusting to the vagaries of the trail. Your stride will shorten and lengthen as you deal with obstacles. Each placement of the foot will be slightly different, engaging muscles all up and down your legs in different ways and through different angles. The strength you develop in these stabilizing muscles will allow you to attack the trail more aggressively, which in turn will further strengthen your legs in a positive feedback loop. The sharper elevation changes you get on a trail will amp up the cardiovascular benefits of the workout as well. You'll have to dig deeper to deal with the steeper gradients of the hills and work harder to master flying down a rough slope without ending up in a face plant.

Moreover, a trail's surface is more forgiving than an asphalt or concrete road. The shock you transmit up through your ankles, knees, and hips with every stride is minimized by the softer surface of a trail, and consequently, you can expect a longer, less injury-prone running career. So with a trail, you get a better overall workout that is less punishing on your body. You also start accruing the benefits of trail running as soon as you step off the road onto a trail.

Moreover, trails are, generally speaking, more aesthetically pleasing than streets and roads. Trails shift your perspective toward the natural world and away from the environment of your workaday world. I've noted many times that one of the more defining things about running is how it can distance you from your normal frame of mind, your social persona, and your everyday concerns. This contrast between what you normally experience and what you experience while running is deepened and made more evident when you exchange a city street for a trail. Out on a trail, that's where the magic happens, where nature is waiting with all her glories. It's like in the musical *Into the Woods*. All the characters are experiencing their "normal" fairytale lives until they venture into the woods. Then all hell breaks loose. The lyrics from one of the musical's songs goes, "You go into the woods where nothing's clear/ Where witches, ghosts and wolves appear/ Into the woods and through the fear/ You have to take the journey."

Out on the trail, or into the woods, is where you go exploring, and that is precisely what you're doing when you run—exploring. You can be exploring your fitness level or exploring how your body is reacting to the miles, or, as this book suggests, you can also be exploring within your mind and discovering how you fit in with the world around you or how the world fits into you.

© Gary Dudney

Venturing into the woods where all the magic happens.

GRENDEL

But let's leave aside any philosophical gobbledygook for a moment and just concentrate on the physical transformation of mild-mannered runner you into a voracious trail monster. It happens little by little, step by step—actually, stride by stride. You step off of the road and onto a trail, and the strengthening begins. In my earlier days of trail running, I was constantly turning my ankle, sometimes badly enough to warrant a trip to the emergency room. But gradually, my ankles strengthened as I persisted on the trails and concentrated on my foot placement. Now when I misstep and turn an ankle, nothing happens. My ankles are strong enough to resist the injury. So I barrel down the trail with that much more confidence.

But having stronger ankles is just a small piece of the larger transformation. The miles of hills turn your hamstrings and calves into steel. The constant dealing with the unevenness of the trail builds tremendous strength in your stabilizing muscles. The greater effort required to handle the vagaries of a trail's surface increases your stamina, especially if you go out for long trail runs. Your dexterity improves from needing to dodge all the obstacles on a trail. You learn to flow down technical sections of the trail, and you learn to pick your way up and over rocks, tree trunks, streams, and less-skilled runners. All the while, you are building confidence in your ability to handle the terrain—to handle any terrain: mountains, forests, deserts, shorelines, or stretches of prairie that extend out to the distant horizon.

Speed is not the issue here, although you might find your times dropping at trail races. The issue is the confidence that you bring to your assault on these trails. You can go long on a long trail, hard on a hard trail, and get through anything that is thrown at you. The more obstacles in your path, the more voraciously you eat them up. You want to fly down that trail like a dragon zooming over the countryside, incinerating anything that gets in its path. You want to wreak havoc in your wake like Taz, the lunk-headed Tasmanian devil in the *Looney Tunes* cartoons. You want to slouch out of the swamp like Grendel, rip open the doors of the mead hall at Heorot, and, with uncontained fury, tear into the sleeping followers of Hrothgar like hell descended upon the damned. You want a trail monster's attitude out there.

HILL TRAINING

Transforming into this ravenous beast is going to happen naturally if you devote enough of your running time to trail running, but there are ways to enhance the process and get you so ramped up that you can step onto the starting line of any race feeling bulletproof. A good place to start the ramping up is with hill training. Hill training pits the body against gravity and can burn up to triple the calories of a flat workout. Running hills provides superior cardiovascular training, and with gravity fighting you every step of the way, lifting your body up all those inclines is great strength training as well. Moreover, the muscles, tendons, and ligaments in your lower body are all strengthened in concert with one another, which is better than working the same muscles independently the way you do with standard weight training.

Make hill training the focus of one or two of your weekday runs to get started or include some hills in a long weekend run. Ideally you should map out a course that gives you about a mile of flat terrain for a warm-up, then a series of three or more climbs, and a final flat mile for your cool-down. Maintain your pace going up the hills but shorten your stride. If the hill becomes very steep, shift into a power walk. Focusing on a strong, steady arm swing can help drive you up the hill. Don't falter near the top of the climb. For maximum benefit, push yourself right over the top before you relax into the downhill. Let gravity work for you as you go back down. Run with a slight forward lean and avoid braking as much as possible. You can control the speed you're generating by using a short stride with a quick turnover. Pick your feet up as soon as they hit the ground. The trip up the hill puts a tremendous load on your hamstrings and calves. The trip down will strengthen your quads.

You can intensify your hill workout by running repetitions up a single slope. Hill reps work like interval training on a track. You alternate running uphill for a specified period of time or distance at a pace that will have you going anaerobic. Then you rest by walking or jogging slowly back down to the start; then repeat. Your level of fitness will dictate how far and fast you go running uphill and how many repetitions you can handle. Hill workouts are intense, so be sure to schedule a rest day afterward to give your muscles a chance to fully recover.

Another way to get the most out of your hill training is to incorporate some exaggerated knee-lifting, bounding drills into your climbs. Pick that point near the top of your climb where you are tempted to slow down and just cruise the rest of the way to the top; instead, steel your quivering loins and bound your way up to the top with 10 to 20 long strides, lifting your knees as high as possible. This technique capitalizes on the built-up fatigue in your legs and pays extra dividends, much like in lifting weights when the last few reps can be worth all the lifts done before them.

Monster trail runners tackling the side of a mesa in Utah.

What if you live in an area devoid of hills? A well-arched bridge or an overpass can serve as your home base for repeats. Running the stairs in a sports stadium makes for an excellent "hill" workout. You can get a similar workout running the stair wells in any tall building or in your hotel while you're on the road. There is also the incline button on your treadmill, or you can use a pre-programmed hill workout built into the machine.

Spend enough time on hills, and you take the teeth out of some of the most difficult race courses out there. Norm Klein, a past race director of the Western States 100 Mile Endurance Run, held the opinion that the number one reason for failure at Western States was due to insufficient training for the long climbs and descents of the race. I've had success and failure at Western States, but the hills were never my problem. In fact, with most of my training done on hilly courses, I look forward to the climbs. In the initial transition from the flat or downhill to the ascent, I feel some strain, but this soon gives way to a feeling that I am settling into the effort and pace. I can feel my strengths coming into play. I convince myself that I am "relaxing" up the hill, and it seems like I get stronger and the effort less onerous the farther up I go. My running partner, who follows the same training routine as I do, has the same success with hills.

Get your own hill-trained inner trail monster runner vibe going and here is what you can expect. Your next race's elevation profile can look like a readout from a Bill Clinton polygraph test, but you will have no anxiety. You will show up at a trail run site which looks, for all the world, like the place where they filmed *The Sound of Music,* but you will feel only calm. You will be able to face some of the biggest uphill starts in trail running at races like Wasatch, Western States, and the Bear, and you will have no fear. You will contemplate the course for the Hardrock 100 in southwest Colorado, and, okay, that will be a little scary, but the point is that your inner trail monster will be wearing a bulletproof jacket when it comes to running hills.

MAKE EVERY RUN AN ADVENTURE

Another technique for developing your inner trail monster is to make your runs into adventure runs. A run becomes an adventure run whenever you get outside the parameters of your usual running workout, and the experience of what you're doing becomes captivating enough or difficult enough that just the running itself becomes secondary. Sometimes this is planned and sometimes not.

You can plan for an adventure run by picking new routes for your runs. A fresh trail or part of town or a new park is always going to be an adventure. Everything along the way will be a new discovery. Instead of expecting to feel a certain way at familiar points along your usual route, you'll be at sea, not knowing exactly how far you've come and how much is left to do. You'll encounter different people and different situations and find new places. You want to make running an all-around enjoyable, captivating experience, not just more miles on the legs. Gong to new places will help that to happen.

You can also choose to run in different conditions than you usually run, even extreme conditions. Instead of avoiding the heat of the day in the summer, go right out in the early afternoon when the sun is most intense and challenge the heat. You'll have to adjust your running, of course, but exploring your limits and seeing what you're capable of in adverse circumstances will be quite diverting for you. Put on plenty of sunblock, wear light-colored clothes, slow your pace, and drink lots of water.

Get out in the rain instead of waiting for clear skies. The smell of the wet earth, the feel of the rain beating down on you, the feel of your damp feet, the look of everything wet and soaked, the rushing streams, and the sound of the rain hitting leaves will overwhelm your senses. A heavy rain is even more thrilling. Astound and impress your couch-bound friends by layering up and going for a run during the next snowstorm. Stay safe. Keep your weight over your feet and be ready to react in case you slip. When everybody else in your climate zone is huddled under comforters, you want to get out there and glory in the zeitgeist of winter. Believe me, as you put your head down into the wind and push over the whited-out landscape while trying to stay upright, the last thing you'll be thinking about is that running can get boring. Incidentally, you should go out into the wind so you can return with the wind at your back.

Your inner trail monster feeds on adversity and grows to meet whatever challenge you bring its way. As you get more skilled at dealing with tough conditions, your attitude about getting out the door on bad days will improve. You want to cultivate that attitude that nothing can stop you; no conditions are too much of a challenge. The greater the adversity, the greater the adventure. You'll be training when others are sitting at home, running miles that others are missing. But you will hardly notice those miles going by; you'll be too busy finding your way along a new route, staying warm in a cold rain, or staving off frostbite.

Another way to spice up your training is to jump into a race. Races are always an adventure. There is the hoopla at the start, all the other runners out there to interact with, the timing, the aid stations if it's a long race, the race site usually chosen for its scenic appeal, and all the perks at the finish line. You can try out new distances. You can switch off road races for trail races, short 5Ks for 50Ks, half marathons for marathons. Don't think that you should only race rarely and that you should have a "target" race that you will only be happy with if you train exclusively for that race, run at the upper limits of your ability, and set a PR. Screw that. Jump into as many races as you want, but think of them as really good workouts. The race format will motivate you to go hard, and the whole thing will be, of course, an adventure.

Look for races in locations out of town where you are traveling. You'll get a close-up look at the environs of your travel destination and probably get a good feel for the locals who you're running with. Consider tackling a whole new type of race like a triathlon, a Spartan race, a multi-day stage race, a mud run, or some other format that includes running and doing something crazy. Feed your inner trail monster these new and different experiences, and it will become lean, sleek, versatile, and unflappable in the face of any challenge.

The quintessential adventure run, in my opinion, is the night run. If you have never run at night, you don't know what you're missing. The darkness transforms everything. It's like finding the magic by going into the woods but on steroids. The most familiar route or trail that you train on all the time will seem strange and full of surprises. Shadows will skitter under your feet. Things will seem to leap at you from the edges of the tunnel of light your flashlight creates. Distances will seem magically shorter or longer. Trail junctions that you never thought twice about will be easy to miss or seem strangely confusing. Different critters are out roaming at night. You might suddenly be sharing the trail with a skunk, have an owl flash by your eyes, or be overwhelmed by a chorus of howling coyotes. And believe me, there's nothing quite as invigorating as pointing your flashlight up onto a bluff above the trail you're running on and seeing a pair of yellow eyes staring back at you.

The night sky is invariably spectacular, especially if you are out in the wilderness away from artificial lighting. Under a full moon, the soft, milky light infuses everything with a magical quality. On a moonless night, the blanket of stars can be stunning. I'll never forget being out in the Flint Hills of eastern Kansas on the tallgrass prairie one night. There were no obstructions, no high ridges, no deep valleys, no rock formations, mountains, pine trees, or manmade structures between me and the great overarching sky. Clouds of glittering stars blanketed the night and extended down to all horizons. Orion seemed close enough to touch with the three perfectly aligned stars forming his belt and the stars of his sword clear and distinct. Just above the horizon in every direction there were scattered lights miles and miles away—the blinking red lights of a radio tower, a bright light bobbing up and down on an oil derrick, a pair of white lights marking a grain silo, and 20 miles away a feint dome of light over the town of Emporia. I had never seen the night sky so full and spectacular in my life. I was running along a jeep road, when suddenly my flashlight lit up the large placid face of a cow right in front of me. I found myself in the middle of a whole herd of cattle that were strung out across the road. No surprise here. I was on a night run. Almost anything could happen.

Adventure runs sometimes happen on their own accord—unplanned and unexpected. You might go out for a little jog from your hotel thinking you'd go out a couple of miles, turn around, and come back. Then you get lost, and your little run turns into a slugfest. I once left my sister-in-law's house on the outskirts of the Polish city of Wroclaw. I was running alone and thought I'd jog over to a nearby town and then come straight back. But the roads wouldn't cooperate, so I'd take a turn and tell myself to remember that one turn, but then I'd have to take another turn and on and on until I'd passed through a bunch of little clusters of houses and small towns, and I was totally lost. Luckily the area was flat farmland, and there was one distinctive church spire that I could see from almost anywhere that I knew was on my way home, so I gave up trying to retrace my steps and just honed in on that spire, and it got me back. My in-laws were scratching their heads and wondering why I'd been running for two hours instead of the 45 minutes I'd promised.

Pleasant weather conditions can turn into a thunderstorm and make your usual Tuesday lunch-hour run on your standard course into a wild, wet adventure. A big windstorm the night before might leave your usual run on a wooded hillside a challenging obstacle course with fallen trees and branches blocking your way at every turn. You might get off on a side trail that you've passed a million times and find yourself bushwhacking across a field of poison oak when the trail peters out or working your way through parts unknown that you never dreamed were there. And every time your usual routine run turns into an adventure run, you get a renewed charge out of running, a new spark to stoke your fire, and your inner trail monster gets to roam a little farther afield.

RUN YOUR OWN TRILOGY

Here is the final suggestion for unleashing your inner trail monster: Make your training something epic. As dedicated trail runners, my running partner and I were thinking in terms of longer and harder trail runs to improve our last month of training, basically late January and February, before the big spring trail races. We'd struggled with this period of time in previous years. It seemed like when we really needed to pour it on, we came up a little stale and uninspired. Just doing more long runs on cold mornings didn't seem that appealing. We needed some kind of massive challenge, something that just by virtue of surviving would be sufficient to get us better trained and ready to face spring. It needed to be like running a gauntlet or a trial by fire. It needed to be epic to capture our imaginations and motivate us to get out the door and onto the frost.

What we did was look at our training over the past couple of years and identify the top quality, most difficult, most demanding training run in our repertoire, which we both readily agreed was a difficult trail run in a local county park that had been dubbed "the VOG" (Victory Over Gary) for reasons that I will not get into but had to do with a friend's fervent desire to grind me into dust when we competed. (I once had a conversation with his innocent five-year-old son. I introduced myself, and he said, "Oh, you're Gary. My dad really wants to beat you!") Anyway, the VOG course was notoriously difficult, with very long and heartbreakingly steep climbs and descents, brutal heat in some open sections, lots of technical sections with tricky footing, and few breaks from the constant elevation change. It took about five hours to cover on a good day and invariably left us drained at the finish.

For our epic training, then, we made the VOG the base. On the first weekend of our big training push, we ran the familiar VOG course, but from a ridge that was the high point of the course, we added an out and back that extended along the ridge off to the west, plunged all the way down to the valley floor, and then returned to the ridge. So to this already demanding trail workout, we added about a six-mile stretch, an extra demanding climb, and about two more hours of running. Then to imbue the whole adventure with the aura of an epic saga, we named this run "The Fellowship of the Rusty Chain." At the bottom of the out-and-back road there was a post with a rusty chain hanging on it. Touching this chain became the ritual act that we shared to mark the occasion of challenging such a difficult training run.

The very next weekend, we ran the VOG again and added yet another tough section to the original course, which followed a very technically difficult trail through a poison oak-infested forest and then up a steep hillside that literally required grabbing on to shrubs to climb to a distant fire tower. At the tower, we ritually touched the door, returned to the point where we'd departed the VOG course, and then went back to the tower again. Of course, in keeping with our Tolkien theme, we called this run "The Two Towers."

© Gary Dudney

Pick rugged, hilly trails to make your own adventure truly epic.

The next weekend, we rested, but we kept up our usual weekday workouts. The idea was to layer the tough, tough series of weekend runs right on top of our regular routine to push ourselves to the max and cement the gains to our stamina and strength. On the weekend after the rest, we jumped into a difficult 50K. We didn't treat the 50K as a race, but rather as just another huge workout, as an extension of our big training effort. And then finally came the pièce de résistance. The next weekend, we completed the final leg of our trilogy series back at the county park. The concept for the final workout, which we called "The Return of the King," was very simple. We ran the whole original VOG course, which took the usual five hours to do. Then we stopped by our cars and wolfed down some food. Then we ran the entire course *again*. At 11 hours, it was the longest self-imposed training run I had ever done in my life. It's hard to overstate how monumental it felt to us to take what had been the very hardest workout we'd ever done and then double it.

Of course, tackling these four difficult runs in just five weeks resulted in building tremendous stamina and endurance. And with all the hill work, our quads were now awesomeness converted to flesh. We'd also faced many of the challenges that we'd be revisiting in the actual races we were planning: rolling out of bed before dawn, running through heat, eating and drinking to keep fueled, facing long climbs on exhausted legs, painful feet, chaffing, and all the other issues which we needed to be prepared for.

Naming the runs, performing our little rituals, doing it together, and specially setting aside time in our calendars to get it all done certainly helped to keep us focused and committed and had the effect of making the effort seem like more than just more training. It imbued the whole enterprise with a certain magic. And like we had set out to do, by just completing the plan and enduring through it, we had significantly improved as runners and stoked the fires underneath our inner trail monsters.

Of course, our program was targeted at extending our endurance for longer and longer trail runs. For someone whose goal is to run a faster 10K, for example, the amped-up training might be something along the lines of additional interval training on a track or a challenging series of tempo runs done at near race pace. A prospective marathoner might schedule a series of more than 20-mile runs over a short period of time or commit to doing a series of back-to-back long runs on successive days. The point is to use your imagination to create a monumental challenge for yourself so that the adventure and romance of meeting that challenge spurs you on to greater feats of running.

In short, trail running offers some clear benefits to the runner, including a well-rounded, coordinated strengthening of the muscles, enhanced dexterity, superior cardiovascular training, reduced wear and tear on the body, and increased resilience to a range of conditions. As these benefits accrue and possibly are sped along by your own targeted efforts—that is, through hill training, adventure running, and making your workouts epic—you can adopt an attitude or a state of mind that you are not just a runner out there being pushed around by the vicissitudes of the trail, but rather you're a frickin' *trail monster*, fully up to any challenge and ready to rumble, and nothing under heaven or on earth is going to stop you!

CHAPTER 9

THE WISDOM
OF CHILLING OUT

One of the great ironies of the sport of running is that the better, smoother, more efficient performance comes not from piling on more effort or more tension, but from being able to relax even as the intensity of the running ratchets up. Even sprinters have to learn to relax during their short, enormously explosive events. They have to distinguish running hard and creating more tension from running efficiently by relaxing and avoiding generating tension.

THE RACING MINDSET

Relaxing is such a key component of performing well that it should be a mindset that you return to over and over again while you are racing. Tension causes your muscles to tighten up, and then you have to actually work against yourself to overcome the tightness. A loose, relaxed body is more efficient, requires less energy to operate, and is better able to move through the range of motion that you are demanding of it.

Race situations just flat out promote tension. The anticipation before the race begins is nerve wracking and enervating. You can feel that carefully husbanded and stored energy that will be crucial during the race draining from your body. At the start you're ready to burst, and like everyone else, you fire off the line and run the first couple of miles way too fast. Once you really begin to register the effort of the run, your reaction is to tighten up with worry and anxiety that comes with knowing what is ahead. When the fatigue really sets in and you begin to struggle, the anxiety can turn to panic. Are you going to record a really poor performance after training so hard? Are you going to fail completely and drop out? Are you going to finish behind runners you usually beat? The panicking results in more anxiety which leads to greater tension which makes it harder and harder to run efficiently, and you spiral downward. You don't enjoy the race much, and when you do finish, you are left feeling unsatisfied and disappointed that you didn't do better.

But just as all the processes that produced this result are mostly in the realm of your mind, the processes that can improve the results are mostly in your mind as well. For every tension-inducing situation, you need to actively counter with techniques and thoughts that will keep you relaxed. A relaxed state of mind will lead to a relaxed body. Prior to the race, you need to create some inner calm. Go through the routine of your preparations and warm up with focus on those activities, not on the coming race. Before the start, find a quiet place, breathe deeply, and force yourself to relax. Shake out the tension and relax your muscles from head to toe, starting at the top and working down. Tell yourself you are trained, you are rested, and you are ready. The outcome will take care of itself. Your job is to stay as relaxed as possible throughout the event.

When the gun goes off, don't burst off the line and sprint for a mile. Chill out. Start the search for a comfortable pace that you can maintain throughout the race. Then relax into that pace. Keep your form, keep your stride efficient, and monitor that you're staying loose. From time to time, bring the thought of staying relaxed back to the center of your attention. Tension can creep up and take hold without your being aware of it. Are your shoulders rising? Are your hands clenched? Does your face feel tight like it's locked into a grimace? Is your breathing going shallow? These are indications that tension is building up. Relaxing your face, your jaw, and the muscles around your eyes will help you relax your whole body. Consciously breathe more deeply and slowly and imagine the tension leaving your body.

As the race goes on and the effort gets more difficult, you need to work even harder to focus on relaxing. No matter how uncomfortable the running becomes, remember that relaxing will make it better; tensing up will make it worse. Direct your attention toward some of the other mental states we've seen in this book, such as staying positive, concentrating on the journey and not the goal, and becoming mindful. Relaxing will follow as your attention shifts away from your discomforts. If you are really struggling, give yourself a chance to rest and recover with a little walking break. Let everything relax. Breathe deeply and shake the tension out of your shoulders, arms, and hands. Pick a spot to walk to, and then when you reach that spot, jog back up to your pace slowly.

© Gary Dudney

The start of a race will always induce tension, and the atmosphere will work against you beginning with a relaxed state of mind.

Another way to stave off the tension is to keep your race in perspective. The race is the reward for getting through all the training and effort it took to get you there. It should be something to be enjoyed, something to savor. How many people are healthy enough and lucky enough to get to line up and run a footrace in their spare time? Relax and just let the race day unfold. Maybe you will succeed and achieve whatever goal you were pursuing, and maybe you won't, but the real triumph was in your preparing to try, and that was accomplished before you took even one step in the actual race. In most cases, nothing substantial is hanging in the balance that will be decided by the results of your race. It is not life or death. Have some fun out there. Being relaxed about the outcome may, in fact, help you turn in your best possible performance.

Running hard and relaxing at the same time is counterintuitive. It takes practice, and your ability to pull it off will improve with practice, so you should not wait until race day to work on the technique. Almost every workout you do will present you with situations in which your natural inclination will be to tighten up, but instead you can practice relaxing. Examples of such situations would include the last 10 or 15 minutes of a tempo run, the final section near the top of a long hill climb, the next to the last and the last repetition of an interval workout, the last few miles of a long training run, or the pick-up sections of a fartlek workout. Monitor yourself for tension any time during any workout and then use the opportunity to focus on relaxing but maintaining the same intensity and speed in your running. Develop a mindset that you are going to go out and accomplish a good workout, and you are also going to relax through it. Develop the habit of relaxing, and it will be familiar and comfortable for you on race day.

DON'T SKIMP ON THE RESTING

It is ironic that relaxing is critical to giving your best performance on race day. It is also ironic that resting is critical to any hard training routines that you might tackle as a runner. The resting you do between runs is just as important as the runs themselves. Becoming a stronger runner involves breaking down and rebuilding muscle tissue. Rob the muscles of their chance to regenerate, and you risk muscle tears, overuse injuries, and permanent damage. So rest days are crucial.

Of course, the bottom line in any running program is going to be how many days on and how many days off you run per week. Many runners gravitate to four and three, meaning four days of running—usually three week days and then either Saturday or Sunday—and three days resting—two of the week days and one day on the weekend. This schedule is fairly relaxed; it gives you a day off after almost every day you run. It involves enough running to allow you to improve if you make some of the workouts more challenging, yet it is not likely to be demanding enough to push you into overtraining or burnout.

Cut out a day of running from this schedule to only three running days a week, and you have a very relaxed program—really, a maintenance schedule. This level of running will allow you to maintain your base fitness, will not lead to overtraining or burnout, and will probably give you stress-free running for years to come. You will not, however, be able to progress much in terms of adding stamina, speed, or distance to your running unless you are doing something unusual like making all three runs long distance or hard speed workouts.

Add a day of running to the typical four-on, three-off weekly schedule so that you are running five days a week and resting for only two, and you are into aggressive training territory. Two days of resting a week may not be adequate for full muscle recovery between workouts, especially if you push each workout fairly hard. Monitor yourself for signs of overtraining. Also add another layer of periodicity to your training by cycling through hard weeks and easy weeks. A typical pattern is to take an easy week after two or three hard weeks of training. So if you are running, for example, five days a week and piling up 50 miles each week, after three weeks of this intensive schedule, take an easy week with an extra couple of days of rest and run no more than half the mileage of the hard week.

Whatever your weekly schedule, be sure to take a rest day after a very intensive workout or after a long run when your need for recovery is greatest. And don't cheat yourself out of a good rest on the rest days. Some walking is fine, but taking an easy run on your rest day defeats the purpose. Also, don't use your rest day for some hard cross-training activity. If you are going to do 20 gnarly miles on your mountain bike, substitute that activity for one of your runs during that week rather than kill the restorative benefits of the rest day. Not enough rest can lead to injury, and injury means you're sitting around not getting to run at all. You don't want to go there.

A lot of runners like to dial back their running for an extended period on a yearly basis—that is, they take a seasonal break from running. Not surprisingly, the seasonal break often corresponds with winter, the holiday season, the worst of the ice and snow, and a period of the year when there are not many organized events going on. A yearly break can do wonders for your attitude about running, especially if you found things getting a little stale. After a long break, your motivation and excitement about getting back on the trails can build and build. You want to avoid, however, stopping your running completely during your long break. A couple of maintenance runs a week will preserve your fitness level and keep you from having to start all over when you resume your training. Or you could go strictly to your cross-training activity during your break and give running a complete rest. The cross-training will preserve your fitness and will leave you eager to get back to running when the break is over.

DON'T SKIMP ON THE TAPERING

A special kind of targeted rest that you will want to employ before racing is called tapering. Tapering is a reduction in your training routine before a targeted event in order to give your body a chance to rest and recover completely from the stresses of training.

The key questions when you are planning your taper are: How long should the taper last; how much should your usual mileage be cut back; and how intense should the running be? The length of the taper is dictated by the goal of giving your body enough time to fully recover from the breakdown process of training, but not so much time that you begin losing the fitness you have worked so hard to obtain. A very common period of time chosen by many runners for a standard taper is three weeks, although it's not uncommon to find runners who try to get by with just two weeks. So your final long run or competing in a "tune-up" race should be done at least two or three weeks before the target event and should represent the last time you seriously push yourself before your big race.

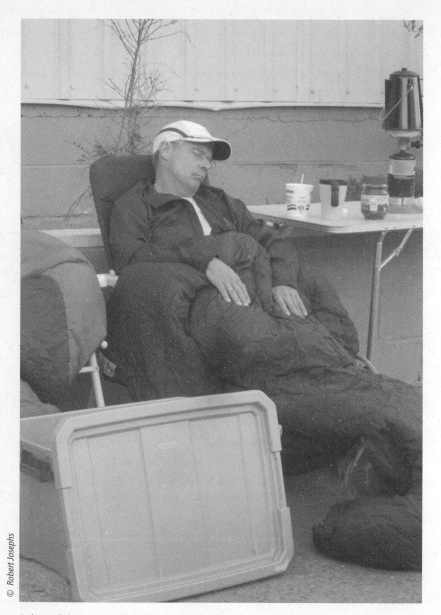

Perhaps a little too much chilling out is demonstrated here.

Your mileage during the first week of a three-week taper should drop by about 30 percent. If your typical training week is 50 miles, for example, dial back to 35 miles. Go for about half your standard mileage in the second week of the taper. In the final week before the race, do a couple of easy runs during the beginning of the week or take the whole last week off completely, although some people like to run a few miles the day before the race to keep their muscles loose. The reduced mileage and especially the final week of almost no running should deliver you to the starting line well rested and bursting at the seams to get running.

How intense should your running be during the taper? Avoid really draining workouts such as interval training, hill repeats, tempo runs, and long runs. Any additional fitness you obtain during these last weeks might be offset by showing up on race day less than fully recovered from the hard effort. Keep to flat courses run at moderate pace. As you cut back your mileage, you can substitute long walks for the workouts you are missing if you are determined to get out the door. Relax during these final runs and enjoy the fact that just jogging along at a very modest pace is, for once, the smart strategy.

In addition to modifying your running during the taper period, there are other things you can do to set yourself up for the best possible result on race day. Get lots of rest and sleep, especially the last few days before the actual run. You may sleep poorly the night just before the race, but that is of no consequence if you've put some extra sleep in the bank. Eat good foods with lots of carbohydrates. Some runners like to refrain from alcohol leading up to a race. Keep yourself well hydrated. Focus on relaxing, but don't be too surprised if you find yourself feeling a little jumpy or you start experiencing odd, phantom pains. Coming off your regular running routine and facing the prospect of the BIG race now that it has finally arrived can trigger a lot of stress. The stress probably explains why some runners actually seem more susceptible to colds and flu while they are tapering. Do your best to keep your thinking positive about the race. Think: "I've trained well; I'm rested and ready; the race will be a big reward for all my hard work."

BEWARE THE SHADOW

Another period for some strategic resting that you would do well to respect is just after a race or after any very draining experience where you have pushed yourself to your limit. I call the time after a race being in the shadow of the race. The longer and harder the race, the longer the shadow extends afterward. For a marathon, I allow for a two-week shadow. A 50-mile race produces a three-week shadow, and there is a full month after a 100-mile race in which I consider myself in the shadow.

Post-race is a time for rest and recovery, although your psychological state may be telling you just the opposite. If the race went well, you feel encouraged and excited about your running. You want to jump right back into hard training so you can ride the wave of success and do even better. If the race didn't go well and you feel discouraged, you might also be motivated to get back out there quickly and "fix" your problem with more hard workouts. So no matter how the race went, instead of giving yourself a solid chance to recover, you instead want to go push it. And that is when you often get injured. When you extend your muscles and connective tissue at that vulnerable time with a hard workout, pulls and tears result.

I respect the shadow by doing no hard or long workouts during the shadow period, cutting my weekly mileage way back, and paying special attention to eating well and getting plenty of sleep. I also do a lot of gentle, careful stretching before each run—about a mile into the run and after the run. If I feel any tightness, tweaks, or especially sore areas while running, I immediately back off and walk or cut the workout short if necessary. Your body will let you know that it's been recently punished. Halfway through the first couple of runs after a race, you can start to feel like you're right back in the race. Workouts that felt easy before the race might feel challenging again. Running two or three days in a row might also feel especially difficult when you're in the shadow.

Your body will also tell you when the shadow passes. You've been struggling with each workout for a couple of weeks, and suddenly a workout goes very smoothly. You feel no residual fatigue in your muscles. You feel energetic near the end of your run, and you never feel yourself dropping down into a more suffering mode. The distance that felt like a stretch a week ago now seems like no problem. Once you start feeling that way, you're ready to resume your training in earnest the following week. You can shift from focusing on the rest you're getting to focusing on pushing yourself once again.

OVERTRAINING AND BURNOUT

Running can be a demanding sport, especially if you're chasing faster times or ramping up to conquer new distances. To improve, you need to get out of your comfort zone. You have to add miles, add tempo, push when you're fatigued, and dig deeper. It's the easiest thing in the world to push a little too far, too fast, and then compound the mistake by not giving your body sufficient time to rest and recover. Persist in this pattern, and eventually you'll start feeling symptoms of overtraining.

Typical signs of overtraining include general fatigue, lingering muscle soreness, restless sleep, irritability, and an elevated resting heart rate. While conditions such as fatigue and muscle soreness are natural reactions to hard training, the overtraining version of these problems persist beyond the point where you would normally recover and bounce back. Even after a decent night's sleep, you might feel drained and achy the next day. When you go out for your next run, instead of feeling energetic and charged up, you toil through the workout, feeling tired and stressed out. A favorite run through the woods that used to be a joy now seems like a chore. You're motivation to get out the door and run drops off a cliff. And despite the seemingly greater effort you put into running, your performance flattens out or even gets worse. You push through a familiar run, running as hard as ever, and you're surprised to find it's taken you a lot longer to finish. What the hell?

The basic remedy for overtraining is more rest. Give your training schedule a hard look. Are you allowing adequate recovery time after your hard workout days and after your long runs? Are you taking just one rest day a week? You might need at least two days or even three. Are you doing too many workouts with high intensity and not enough easy, recovery workouts? Are you piling up a string of high-mileage weeks without occasionally cycling in an easy week with reduced mileage? Are you sticking to your workout plan with no regard to how you feel? Sometimes your body lets you know it's time to rest. Pay attention. Avoid doing junk miles when a good rest might be a lot more beneficial. Give yourself a thorough break after a hard race effort. You might be motivated to dive back into a harder than ever routine, but let your body recover first and ramp back up slowly. With more rest in your training schedule, you should feel the overtraining symptoms fade and your enthusiasm for running return.

The other condition that runners often experience is burnout. Burnout seems to be more a mental than a physical issue. It usually results from following an unvaried routine of continuous training and racing until running becomes very stale, repetitive, and uninspiring. It leads to you feeling very apathetic about training and racing. You feel reluctant to set new goals. You find excuses for skipping runs and keeping races off your calendar. The perceived drudgery of running trumps in your mind all the reasons you used to enjoy running. Having met the initial goals that you set when running was fresh, you move on to other interests, and before you know it, you're hardly running at all.

Since burnout usually results from getting stuck in a rut and growing tired of the same old routines, workouts, and races, overcoming burnout involves changing things up. First, try getting more rest. Maybe your burnout is linked to long-term overtraining fatigue. Cut back for a while on the workouts that can be really daunting and stressful, like difficult long runs, tempo runs, and speed work. Change up your mix of hard and easy runs and rest days. Seek out some different running routes and different terrain. Invite some new running partners along. Try taking a break from running altogether and see if your motivation doesn't return all by itself once you've had some time away from running.

Finally, don't get down on yourself for feeling burned out. Shit happens. It's easy to overdo any good thing. You were trying hard, and maybe it got to be just a little too much. Take a break and then work back into it slowly. You'll probably end up learning something useful about your training and how running best fits into your life.

THE YIN AND THE YANG OF THE BIG CHILL

Relaxation and effort, resting and training—these are the yin and yang of running, seemingly contrary entities that are actually complementary and work together harmoniously. We tend to focus on the effort of running and the training that we put in and take the relaxation and the resting for granted. But let the system get out of balance, ignore the relaxation and resting too much, and you will likely fall short of your potential and risk injury, overtraining, and burnout. Find the harmony between effort and relaxation and between training and resting, and the running will stay vibrant, enlivened, and rewarding.

So here is the plan. Take a hard look at your training and racing habits. Have you built in plenty of rest and recovery time in your schedule? Do you periodically give yourself a chance to just recuperate and not push harder all the time to reach a higher level of training? Do you take long breaks from running in the winter or spend some time cross-training to give your body a break from running all the time? Be conscious of the value of the rest that you get. Appreciate it and enjoy it.

And when you train, make relaxing a focus of the process. Learn to respond to the tougher parts of the workout with more relaxation, with shedding more tension. Then when you race, chill out.

THE WISDOM OF CHILLING OUT

CHAPTER 10

LEADVILLE AGAIN

Back in Leadville and our conquest of the Grand Slam of Ultrarunning, I had not seen Robert since shortly after the race began when I could have sworn he ran up a hill that I was walking and then disappeared into the distance ahead of me. I caught no glimpse of him all the way to May Queen, the first aid station on the course, and likewise saw nothing of him all the way over Sugarloaf Pass. My crew at the Fish Hatchery aid station had had no contact with his crew, so there was no news there, either. I concluded that Robert was having a strong race and that his fear that he would not do well in the thin air of Leadville had turned out to be unfounded.

At Twin Lakes, which was 40 miles into the race going out, my crew had still not had any word of Robert. I figured I'd catch him going up to Hope Pass, but the whole climb and descent went by without a sign of him. When I got to the bottom of the trail and turned onto Clear Creek Road, heading for the turnaround at Winfield and the 50-mile mark of the race, my crew was waiting with the news. I had been mistaken all along. Somehow I'd gotten out in front of Robert in the first five miles of the race. Comparing notes later, Robert said he'd seen me go by and told me to have a good race, but I must have been completely lost in my own world.

The real story, I found out, was that Robert had stayed close behind, reaching May Queen only a few minutes after I left. After that he steadily lost ground and in fact was discovering that his previous unhappy experience at altitude was playing itself out once again. At Twin Lakes, he was feeling the pressure of the cutoffs. It would have been an easy decision to call it quits right there without tackling Hope Pass. After all, he was not in the running for the Grand Slam anymore and was mostly there to support me and keep my hopes alive. The possibility of a finish looked very remote. He had come to the conclusion that the altitude was just too much of a barrier for him, even under the best of circumstances. But in typical fashion for him, he pressed on.

© David Nakashima

Robert standing in back helping two of us through a self-supported run in Southern California.

Meanwhile, I was leaving the turnaround at the halfway point at Winfield with my huge safety margin of time for covering the last 50 miles and already anticipating knocking out the whole Grand Slam. There was just one seemingly insignificant, little, annoying problem: Things were not all dandy in ankle world. That minor little pain that I'd had in the front of my ankles in the first 10 miles of the race had been steadily increasing in intensity. I'd gone to my painkillers early on, keeping the problem well under control. But as I cruised along the road that would take me back to the trailhead leading up to Hope Pass, I was starting to register higher levels of discomfort, and it seemed like the painkillers had lost their magic punch. In fact, they didn't seem to be doing diddly-squat. I decided to give myself a break and walk the two miles back to the trailhead. I'd be cashing in a little of my safety margin, but taking a break felt wonderful and walking was easier on the ankles.

The climb back up to Hope Pass was slow and tedious, but I figured once I'd gotten over the top I'd be blitzing down the other side of the pass and flying into Twin Lakes at 60 miles, heading home with most of my time cushion intact. I met Robert very close to the top of the pass coming the other way. It was already past the cutoff time for his next aid station, so he was out of the race, but he was pleased to have at least conquered Hope Pass and was counting the day as a success.

Not but a couple of minutes after seeing Robert, I crested Hope Pass and immediately got a very unhappy surprise. Running downhill was torture. The little bit of extra stretching at the top of my ankles that the downhill camber of the trail was causing was unbearable. My plans to fly down the other side of Hope Pass went up in smoke. I was back to walking—and very gingerly at that. I made it down to the aid station where I had some soup and coffee and watched the llamas chewing grass. They seemed pretty indifferent to my problems. I glanced into a nearby tent and saw two volunteers huddled over a runner with shaggy hair who was slumped in a chair.

"Is that…?" I started to ask a woman who was taking a cup of soup into the tent.

"Yes," she said. "It's Chlouber. He's past the cutoff."

So Chlouber himself had been cut down. It seemed a bad omen.

I stumbled and nursed my ankles all the way down from Hope Pass to the valley below. When I finally got to the river just before reaching Twin Lakes, I waded in and stood there, hoping the cold water would numb my ankles. I was surprised to see Hans-Dieter Weissharr just up ahead of me. He was a retired German doctor who traveled all over the States in a big RV doing 100-mile races. In other races we'd been in together, he was usually well out ahead of me. I asked him how we were doing, and he said, "I have been right here in the dark, and I finished." It was still light out, so that made me feel secure that things were still well in hand.

Nevertheless, at Twin Lakes, I checked my time, and I was definitely cutting into my safety margin. All the walking was taking its toll on my pace. I'd read that it was possible to walk all the way to Leadville from the turnaround and still finish, but that assumed a strong, fast, relentless walk. My walking was better described as weak, slow, and give-me-a-break.

On the trail over to the next aid station, Halfmoon, runners were catching and passing me all the time. I so envied the ease with which they moved along, most of them in an easy comfortable looking jog. I couldn't hang with even the slowest of them. I'd try to break into a shuffle, but then the pain would demand attention, and I'd slouch back into walk mode. Chlouber had said to make friends with pain, but I felt like I'd married pain, had kids with it, worked my whole life to put bread on the table, and was ready to retire. I wanted a divorce.

The aid station tent at Halfmoon was full of struggling, beat-up runners like me. I was exhausted. I asked one of the volunteers to wake me up in 10 minutes, and I tried closing my eyes, but I was too uncomfortable to fall asleep. There was nothing to do but get back on the road and engage the pain. As I crept along, runner after runner went by me, just about everyone that I had seen at Halfmoon. Most of them were walking, but I was amazed at how much better they were moving than me and how quickly they disappeared ahead of me. When I got on the last stretch of road leading up to the Fish Hatchery, I looked back into the valley I'd just crossed, searching for flashlights behind me. I could see probably two or three miles of the course from where I was, and there was not a single light in sight. My heart sank. I had lost so much time that now I was possibly bringing up the rear of the runners still in the race. I tried to fight off total despair, but I felt like I was in the ring with a guy who had anvils in his gloves.

That was how I came to be on the cot at the Fish Hatchery where Kathy found me. I had been running through the pain for hours and hours, all the time trying to hide from the fact that I might be injured and that the correct action would be to stop. But I would not only be giving up on a finish at Leadville for the second time, but the Grand Slam as well. Avoiding that crushing disappointment had kept me going, but coming into the Fish Hatchery and seeing that I might be dead last and therefore very unlikely to make the final time cutoff anyway, suddenly the wisdom of stopping won out, and I took to the cot. But Kathy had stirred up the still hot embers of my Grand Slam fire before it was extinguished completely, and I was now standing at the bottom of the climb to Sugarloaf, cursing Robert with all my heart.

THE END OF THE TRAIL

I took maybe five steps up the Sugarloaf Pass ascent and came to a dead stop. I could barely move. The exhaustion, the hours of dealing with the pain, the climb, and the thought that I was almost certainly not going to make it to May Queen in time all came crashing down on me. But just then I was surprised by four runners coming up from behind. So I wasn't last after all. Hans-Dieter was one of them. Earlier I'd seen him at an aid station, lashing a bag of ice to his swollen ankle. The bag was still there, and he was moving fine. He told me to join his group and assured me we could still make it. I tried to hang on to them for a while—my last hope—but I couldn't do it. I watched them glide away up the hill. I knew I needed to be moving like that to finish, but I wasn't, and all the determination in the world wasn't going to change that simple fact.

In order to drop, I had to go about 10 more miles to May Queen over Sugarloaf Pass, which I physically could not do, or turn around and retrace the mile back to the Fish Hatchery. I turned around. I let go of Leadville, and I let go of the Grand Slam. My summer was over. I limped back to the road. Kathy and her car were long gone. I turned toward the Fish Hatchery. In just one mile, or in about 30 minutes, I would be back on that marvelous cot. My screaming ankles would be elevated. A kindly volunteer would be feeding me soup and solace.

The mile seemed to stretch on and on. I came to what I remembered as the last bend in the road before the aid station, but there was nothing ahead—no lights, no nothing. The night was very dark. I could just make out a white pickup pulling onto the road not too far ahead of me and speeding off. I walked on a bit and then realized with a shock that I was standing right next to the aid station, but it was deserted. All the lights in the big garage building that had been the aid station were off.

The medical tent where my cot was supposed to be was gone. I couldn't believe it. When I left, the place was a beehive of activity—people everywhere, cars everywhere. There must have been a mad rush to pack up and get out of there after the last runners came through, the group with Hans-Dieter. The pickup that I'd just missed turned out to be the very last vehicle leaving the place. It had never even occurred to me that the aid station would be shutdown. I was totally screwed.

I limped around the place, searching for signs of life in one of the cars or campers that were parked there. I tried the doors on the buildings. Everything was locked up tight. Moreover, it was four in the morning, and the mountain air was turning cold. Now that I wasn't moving, I was getting chilled to the bone. The one great thing about quitting was supposed to be that you could finally lie down and find comfort on a cot, in the back seat of a heated car, or even back in a luxurious hotel room. I was standing in the dark and the cold and tired and hurt as I had ever been in my life, and there was nowhere to go and nothing that I could do. I sat down on the curb of the road and fought back the urge to start crying in frustration.

I was there for about 20 minutes when I thought I saw headlights turn off a road that was about a mile away and head toward me. The lights disappeared into a low spot, and my heart sank in my chest, but then they popped back up, still coming in my direction. I stepped into the middle of the road and got my flashlight ready. I was either going to flag this car down or die under its wheels.

"Yeah, I can take you into Leadville," Tim Roy from New Hampshire said. He was also a grand slammer. He'd stepped into a hole near Twin Lakes and messed up his Achilles tendon, so he was also out of the Slam. He'd come out to the Fish Hatchery to pick up his drop bag. He dropped me off at the finish line where I had to repeat my story three or

THE TAO OF RUNNING

four times before someone who could officially cut off my wristband heard me out. I had a message radioed out to my crew at May Queen, and then it was up to me to walk over to the hotel.

Robert let me in the door to our room. "Now we're both done," I said and dropped onto bed.

Neither of us went to Wasatch for the final leg of the Grand Slam. I had the ankle problem, and Robert had had enough of high-altitude, 100-mile races. An orthopedic surgeon and a physical therapist who specializes in the biomechanics of the foot both diagnosed my ankles. They agreed that I had an unusual case of acute tendonitis affecting the tibialis anterior ligament which runs across the ankle and attaches the muscle on the lower outside of my leg to the inside bottom of my foot. They also determined that the band of fibrous tissue that runs across the ankle and aligns and holds the tendons that go down into the foot in place was also inflamed. The therapist told me that if I had persisted in running and wrecked that band, I might have blown my whole running career for good. I could have kissed him when he said that.

BACK TO LEADVILLE...YET AGAIN

I'd failed at the Grand Slam. The back-to-back-to-back races had just been too much for my ankles. But once I was recovered, it seemed like Leadville by itself was within my grasp, and her siren call was, to me, deafening. I came roaring back with a couple of solid 50Ks the next spring followed by a decent American River 50 mile and then a good time at the Miwok 100K. I figured I was in at least as good a shape as I'd been the year before during the Grand Slam attempt, and this time I would be tackling Leadville fresh without the drag of two 100s in the weeks before the race. I knew the course inside and out, knew I could run at altitude, and knew I could have finished if I'd been free of the ankle problem. *This year there would be no surprises,* I thought.

The race orientation for 2004 in the Sixth Street Gym was beginning to feel like home. There was Chlouber pacing before the crowd, Merilee at his side. Aron Ralston was back as an official runner this time. His previous race experience outside the pacing at Leadville apparently had been just one 5K race, but I don't think there was anyone in the gym who doubted he would finish. Bill Finkbeiner was there going after buckle number 21. He'd felt good at the 20-buckle milestone, so he'd decided to begin his quest for 30 consecutive Leadville finishes.

The four o'clock shotgun blast the next morning was old hat to me, as was the rush down Sixth Street to get out of town and onto the Boulevard toward Turquoise Lake. At the 10-mile mark, I took stock: breathing easily, good pace, no surprise aches or pains, and blessed silence from my ankles. On the trail just beyond May Queen, which features a jumble of shin-banging rocks and boulders, a guy running nearby kept tripping and falling. I felt so chipper, I tried out some humor. "Oh, I get it, the *Rocky* Mountains," I said. The ensuing silence ended my comedy aspirations for the day.

A light rain in the valley below Hope Pass turned into a heavy rain and lightning as we climbed higher. Gale-force winds threatened to carry the aid station tents off at the top of Hope Pass. On the back side of the pass, several sections of trail had turned into muddy slippery slides. I made it down and out to the turnaround at Winfield 10 minutes ahead of my time from the previous year. Again, I would be tackling the last 50 miles with a comfortable margin. The big difference was that I'd had no nagging ankle problem dogging me all day this time around.

Back at the Hope Pass aid station, the wind had died down. I was ready for a little break, so I took my soup over to a large stone and had a seat. Gradually, a strange sensation crept over me that I was being watched. I looked up and found a llama placidly staring at me from just a few feet away. The infinitely suffering and marvelously patient look on the llama's face somehow bucked up my resolve. It was like the opposite of Chlouber stoking up our emotions with talk of grim determination and grit. My llama Zen master seemed to be holding out another path. Go smoothly and peacefully on your path, it seemed to be saying, seek enlightenment as you run. I finished my soup, strapped on my belt, and sought my destiny down the mountain.

The night came on as I passed back through Twin Lakes. The stars came out. The cold air was bracing. I jogged along comfortably and walked when I felt like resting. My pace tracked with my race plan perfectly, and the miles took care of themselves. Beyond Sugarloaf Pass on the road leading to May Queen, I looked up at the brilliant stars. Orion glittered just above the ridge I had just descended. Lights from other runners zigzagged down the ridge toward Turquoise Lake. It was very beautiful and serene.

I passed through May Queen elated that I was just 13 miles from the end. I had plenty of time and no worries. But this was Leadville, and Leadville was not going to give up without a fight. I had been sort of wheezing since way back at Twin Lakes, but it hadn't slowed me down any. Now whenever I took a deep breath, it brought on a cough. And strangely, I couldn't seem to finish a sentence without stopping to catch my breath.

The final roads leading up to Leadville seemed all uphill now, and the warming sun started to punish me. I was overdressed from the night. I'd passed up the last chance to dump my excess clothes at May Queen.

I pushed on, always hoping to catch a glimpse of town around the next corner, but it refused to appear. And now I had to stop regularly and bend over and take several deep breaths just to keep going. I had no idea what was happening. After dealing with the altitude just fine, it was suddenly unbearable.

"I CAN'T BREATHE"

I'd slowed to a crawl by the time I had topped the rise on Sixth Street just out of town. I could see the finish line and the crowd gathered at the sides of the road and beyond the finish banner. I ran down and then walked up the last block. The crowds on either side were clapping for me. I stepped across the finish line and on this, my third try, finally completed my journey. Merilee O'Neal slipped a ribbon with a finisher's medal dangling from it over my head, and I got my long-awaited hug. I felt Ken Chlouber pat me on the back. I looked at Merilee and said, "I can't breathe."

I was taken directly to the medical tent and put down on a cot. A nurse clipped an oximeter to my finger and found my blood oxygen level was well below normal. The staff in the medical tent all agreed I should go straight to the hospital. I could see my friends peeking into the tent from outside, wondering what the heck was going on. Why wasn't I dancing around with glee at having finished?

The nurse helped me get up, and I staggered outside. "We're going... (gasp for breath)...to the hospital," I said.

© Rob Mann

The family support system that allowed me to go off to Leadville over and over again, from left to right: me, my daughter Anna, my wife Grazyna, and my son Arthur... all runners.

Before long, the doctor was explaining high-altitude pulmonary edema to me and listing off all the symptoms which I had been experiencing in the last 10 miles of the race. In short, my lungs had been filling up with fluid, and I was on my way to drowning. Some people are just prone to HAPE, and others are not. I was, or at least, I was when I ascended to high altitude rapidly and then tried to run for 30 hours.

The remedy was high doses of oxygen and descent to lower altitude. I sat in the hospital bed in my dirty running clothes, my legs covered with dust and grime, with the oxygen tubes shoved up my nose for one hour after another. By the time I could say a whole sentence without gasping for breath, I was getting claustrophobic and wanted out of there. I also wanted to make the awards ceremony back in town, but the doctor wouldn't release me. Eventually, I talked him into renting me a portable oxygen supply, and we rushed out of there with me lugging a big silver cylinder of oxygen along.

The ceremony was over by the time we got to the Sixth Street Gym, but people were still milling about. I spotted Merilee. I explained to her what had happened. She rummaged through some boxes and produced a belt buckle and a sweatshirt that had my name printed on the sleeve along with my finishing time, 29:08:26. I clutched them to my chest and thanked her profusely. I found out later, by the way, that Aron Ralston had also finished somewhere behind me. Of course, we'd missed seeing the crowd's reaction to him coming forward to receive his rewards.

My crew and I left immediately for Denver. I sat in the passenger's seat with my buckle, my sweatshirt, and my cylinder of oxygen in my lap. From time to time, I would remove the tubes from my face and see how well I was breathing without the oxygen. Shortly after reaching Denver, I was breathing normally again.

THE TAO OF RUNNING

On the plane ride home, I watched the Rocky Mountains pass beneath me. For three years I had been coming to the Rockies as if in search of my destiny. Now I was done. I no longer needed to go back to Leadville; actually, I felt like I never wanted to see Leadville again as long as I lived. I had the finisher's belt buckle with me on the plane. I pulled it out of my backpack. It came in a little white box nestled in a bed of cotton. I opened the box and stared at the buckle. I thought, *What does this mean?*

© Anna Dudney

Sebastian and Hermes react to the news back home that I finally finished at Leadville.

CHAPTER 11

RUNNING AS AN EXISTENTIAL EXPERIENCE

What did my Leadville buckle mean? Surely that was a legitimate question after all I had been through to get it: three long expensive trips to Colorado, hundreds of miles of gnarly training runs, excruciatingly painful failures, ankle injuries, and a brush with mortality at the hands of high-altitude pulmonary edema.

I thought of Pam Reed appearing on David Letterman's show. She was fresh off her second win at the 135-mile Badwater UltraMarathon—a race that begins at 282 feet below sea level in California's Death

Valley, where temps can reach into the 130s, and ends at Whitney Portal, the trailhead to Mount Whitney at 8,360 feet. Reed pliantly and straightforwardly responded to Letterman's questions, some of which were obviously designed to make Reed seem like a loon. Letterman chuckled along, shaking his head at the absurdity of what she was saying. The ultimate question designed to highlight Reed's—what?— gullibility was when he asked what she earned for her efforts.

"A belt buckle," Reed said.

This response, of course, spawned one of Letterman's taken aback, turn to the audience, pregnant pauses, after which, he said, "Well, good lord, sign me up. Where do I get in on this? A *new belt buckle*, are you kidding me?"

I passed a finger over the shiny silver surface of my freshly won buckle. The convex surface of the buckle was beautifully chased with fan-shaped indentations, wriggling coils that snaked across the surface and around the edge, and teardrop-shaped accents angling off the coils. I closed my eyes. And now that I look back on that moment, I wonder if the woman sitting next to me on the plane that day noticed the weirdo in the seat next to her, dreamily fingering a belt buckle instead of watching the inflight movie.

© Gary Dudney

Perhaps this sign maker was making an existentialist statement.

PAYING ATTENTION TO THE JOURNEY

Whatever her impression, I closed my eyes and took stock. Had anything in my running come to an end with at last finishing Leadville? Not really. I'd long ago internalized the insight I'd gotten from *Rocky*. I hadn't been focused on the buckle so much. I'd been paying attention to the journey I was on and how running was transforming my life.

186

And what a journey! All the places I'd been to, all the friends I'd made, all the things I'd seen, all the really spectacular and the really crappy situations I'd gotten into on those endless trails. All the mini goals along the way that I'd set and conquered.

Physically, there was no doubt I'd gotten stronger and much more durable. My quads were like steel. I could climb anything without getting fatigued. In fact, I'd feel stronger near the top of a climb, almost as if the slower pace going up was more restful than taxing. During a long run, if I ran within myself and kept the pace moderate, it felt like I could run forever as long as I kept the calories coming and all my fluids topped up.

As far as mental toughness, I'd made strides as well. When things got difficult, I could count on working some of Dahlkoetter's psychological jiu-jitsu and seeing the positive in even the worst physical sensations I was experiencing. I had mantras ready and waiting to keep myself focused on the task at hand and short circuit negative thoughts before they undermined me. I knew how to get myself completely relaxed even when I was feeling at my worst. And I was getting better and better at using mindfulness to stay in the moment, approach my thoughts and sensations with a certain objective detachment, and avoid letting negative things from the past or worries about the future influence my ability to deal with the present.

These incremental improvements in my ability to deal with the vicissitudes of running and racing were just part of the picture. Running had gradually insinuated itself more centrally into my life. In days past, like when I'd become fed up with chasing faster 10K times, I was ready to give it up altogether, maybe move on to tennis or, God help me, golf. I'd needed the heady goal of pursuing my first marathon finish to get me back into running mode. But now I realized knocking out the big silver buckle from Leadville was barely a blip on my running horizon. It wasn't *if* I was going to come up with a new running goal; it was which of a dozen new and exciting running goals was I going to pick and would I settle on one before my flight from Denver touched down in California.

I realized I had become committed to running—hook, line, and sinker. It wasn't just how I happened to exercise. It wasn't just what I did with my spare time. It was an integral part of me. I had become passionate about it. It had become a *passionate commitment*.

GETTING OUT OF BED

Here's just one example. I am not the world's most spectacular morning person. Left to my own devices, I would probably get in bed at two in the morning every day and get up at ten o'clock, having happily missed the sunrise, breakfast, and the annoyingly cheerful, energetic, overachieving early birds that always get the worm, which they can keep for all I care, by the way. Unfortunately, the vast majority of the human population won't cooperate with my preferred schedule, so most mornings of my life, I have bucked my natural inclinations and gotten out of bed at a decent hour.

Of course, I have no choice on race mornings but to get up at an ungodly hour, but most of my training miles are done late morning or in the afternoon. My latest running buddy, Rob (Rob Mann, not to be confused with Robert Josephs), and I usually meet at lunchtime for our run, but not long ago, he hatched an evil plan to come by my house every Tuesday early in the morning before work so we wouldn't miss a day when he had to work over lunch. Soon I was cancelling this run on a regular basis, according to any flimsy excuse I could lay my hands on. But when it was revealed that one morning I had begged off the run because I preferred staying in bed another hour and taking a hot shower, it became Rob's cause célèbre. Now I can break both legs and have pneumonia, but if I try to get out of a run, he will claim I am bugging out because I would rather take a hot shower.

From time to time, Rob would succeed in getting me to run early on weekends. One Sunday morning run, in particular, caught my attention. We'd settled on our old standard route in a park in Carmel Valley called Garland Ranch—the VOG. It was hilly, very difficult, five hours long, and as familiar as the back of my hand. There was nothing about it that made it stimulating, just the prospect of five-plus hours of sheer punishment. It happened to be the dead of winter, possibly the longest night of the year, and when the alarm went off at five so I could meet Rob at the park by six, I was not a happy camper. The last thing I wanted to do was get up and run some more.

Nevertheless, there was no question that I was going to meet Rob, and an hour later, I was shivering in the dark in the frosty air in the parking lot at Garland Ranch, trying to loosen up my legs and stuff the last of my supplies into my hydration pack. We hiked around to the visitor's center and then very stiffly and painfully shifted into a jog along the valley floor on what is called Lupine Loop. Initially, my fingers were freezing, and I longed for a thicker jacket and a woolen cap instead of my flimsy running hat, but from long experience I knew that I'd warm up eventually and then be stuck carrying the extra useless clothes around for five hours.

And it wasn't like having overcome all that inertia in bed, the winter morning, the lack of any interest in this run, the cold drive over to the park, and the stiff painful start, we were somehow home free. The course ahead of us was virtually unbroken steep climbs and descents, rough trail, and no comfort. One climb beyond the halfway point of the run we called "visiting Shit City" because it always made us feel exquisitely awful no matter how well the run was going otherwise. So as we jogged along in the crisp air, the Carmel River on our left and the frosty valley floor on our right, and with the ridge that we were repeatedly going to climb looming above us, I had an epiphany and thought, *I must love this running thing very much.*

How to explain this love of what I was doing, this passionate commitment? Some people find running boring. Not me. Quite the contrary, most of the time I spend running, I'm enthralled with the whole experience. Running seems to put me on a different plane from other areas of my life. It makes me feel uniquely alive. When I run, I feel most genuine within my own skin, most fully myself. The reason I feel that way, and why many other runners feel something similar, may be explained, I believe, by looking at the philosophy of existentialism.

SARTRE AND COMPANY

Existentialism! That sounds pretty forbidding, doesn't it? Wasn't that some kind of atheistic philosophy that burned out in the last century? It was, indeed, all the rage in the 20th century post World War II. And some prominent existentialist philosophers, notably Jean-Paul Sartre, who named the existentialist movement and popularized it, were atheists, but in contrast, an earlier philosopher who is considered foundational to the philosophy, Soren Kierkegaard, was, in fact, a deeply devout Christian.

What remains relevant about existentialism is that it asks some very fundamental questions about the meaning of life and how to conduct one's life. It has much to say about the topics of individuality, freedom, choice, self-improvement, and self-realization, which is why it had such a major impact on thinking in the United States where these topics, in particular, have traditionally been of such interest.

Existentialist philosophy posits that meaning in life derives from one's individual existence and the choices that one freely makes in living one's life. In other words, what we are or what we become is essentially up to each of us individually. We are free to choose our path in life, and with that freedom comes responsibility. Existentialists reject the notion of some outside authority dictating our actions or fate. We, alone, are responsible for what we become and collectively for how the world is because the nature of the world results from our choices. Existentialism has been called the philosophy of "no excuses." We can't blame God for how the world is or nature or some force determining the direction of history. We must look to ourselves for the responsibility.

Sartre captures one of the main tenants of existentialism in his phrase, "existence precedes essence." For an individual, this means that existing in the world is the fundamental experience of human life, and out of this existing and how you chose to handle it comes your essence—that is, the person you become. And it should be noted that by "existence" we mean all the totality of your situation in the world; your time and place of birth; your interactions with all the people around you; and all your own emotions, sensibilities, sensations, thoughts, and feelings. All these things are part of your existing in the world and influence your choices and how you work to define yourself.

So what does this existentialist notion of life have to do with running in particular? There are two ways, it seems to me, in which an existentialist view of the world seems closely aligned with the act of running. One is the very act of choosing to run in the first place, selecting running to pursue as an activity out of the universe of possibilities for how you could spend your time. The other way is found in the nature of running itself and how you tend to engage directly and fully with the world around you when you run in all your capacities — that is, physically, mentally, and emotionally.

CHOOSING TO RUN

In his essay entitled "La Republique du Silence" in 1944, Sartre famously wrote concerning the experiences of the French during World War II, "We [the French people] were never more free than during the German occupation." Surely only an existentialist could write a line like that and have it somehow make sense. But it relates to the philosophy's emphasis on having the absolute freedom to choose how one lives one's life. Everyone is surrounded by a multitude of perceived dictates about what one should do with one's life and how to behave. If your mother was a lawyer, you might feel compelled to follow in her footsteps. If your father practices strict Catholic ritual, you might feel that in worshipping God you must do the same. Society places a myriad of expectations on how you should act, talk, dress, interact with others, and feel about the world. It's easy to concede to all these norms and simply go along with what is expected of you. But the existentialist asks you to consider each decision and make a willful choice according to what seems true to you as an individual. Are you really excited by the prospect of practicing law? Do your religious impulses really conform to your father's?

© Gary Dudney

We choose to run; and that gets us out in the wide world and away from all the distractions

Friedrich Nietzsche describes the pressure to conform to the norms of one's society as being part of the "herd" and criticizes this way of thinking as being antithetical to discovering your true self. As long as you continually allow your choices to be dictated by what helps you simply fit in with and go along with the flow, your choices are unlikely to help you become your true, authentic self. Authenticity is another related concept and is central to Martin Heidegger's ideas about how one should conduct one's life. An authentic life is one in which we have "taken ahold of ourselves," that is, we have actively made choices to become who we really are, to live up to our potentials, to follow our own path versus simply going along with the herd.

Which brings us back to what Sartre meant in saying that the French were never so free as when the Nazis were in charge. The ability to simply live from day to day, conforming to all the norms of French society, and not being particularly thoughtful about one's life was stripped away during the occupation. Every French individual was faced with making a choice—one could say, an existential choice. You could collaborate; you could resist; or you could attempt to ignore the Nazi presence. The choice you made was going to be deep and consequential. There was no option for simply living your life and not really confronting who you truly were.

So in the existentialist's world, choosing to run is freighted with meaning, especially since it represents a free choice on your part, probably not coerced out of you by some societal dictate or by some overarching belief system. You just choose to run out of some notion that it will make you a better, fitter person. And if you run enough, you will probably be surprised at just how much better and fitter you become as a person. You might notice, as many runners do, that you feel singularly alive while you're running and that you get a very profound sense of satisfaction out of it. The existentialist would explain that, in choosing to run, you have made a step toward self-actualization, toward becoming who you really are, and it feels pretty great.

BEING IN THE WORLD

Existentialism takes its name from "existence" because the philosophy elevates purely existing in the world above all other influences on who we are and what gives life meaning. But in going about our lives, we are so caught up in the drama of our jobs, our relations, our material situation, and the like that we hardly notice many of the more fundamental components of being here in the world. That is, until we go out and run.

Running makes us intensely aware of our physical existence. In fact, while running, we are flooded with our physical existence. We feel all the strains on our bodies. We pass through a kaleidoscope of sights, sounds, and smells. We encounter the warmth or coolness of the air; the wind against our skin; the changing elevation of the land; and the variety of open fields, woods, city blocks, manicured parks, or dusty roads where we're running. We experience using our bodies to achieve this continuous motion very directly and how our bodies respond to the challenge.

Consider for a moment just what a break your 20-minute or hour-long run provides from your normal activities. It's like a paradigm shift from the rest of your day. You switch clothing, and suddenly you are deep inside a physical activity and overwhelmed with the sensory impressions of the world around you. Mentally, you step out of whatever roles you normally fulfill—be it mother, wife, father, husband, dutiful coworker, attentive salesperson, sympathetic supervisor, or omnipotent professional. You can drop the masks you might be wearing, set aside the persona you are projecting, and ditch your ego. What good do any of those do you out running, anyway? The trail doesn't care if you're meeting your sales quota or giving enough attention to your mother-in-law or pretending to be somebody you're not.

All the constant pater of your overbearing consciousness can quiet down, leaving you space to just exist, to just be, and to just take in the world unimpeded. Some existentialists hold a rather dim view of consciousness to begin with. An oft-cited example is what sometimes happens to people attending a classical music concert. You get all duded up and go sit in this magnificent auditorium. The atmosphere is charged with pomp, circumstance, and culture. After a tension-filled pause and the annoying rustling sounds picked up by the mics as the musicians lift their instruments, the dramatic first chords of the music swell up from the stage. Almost at once, you become acutely aware of the process of listening to the music. You know you are supposed to let yourself go, to lose yourself in the music, but instead you become more and more conscious of thinking about properly listening to and appreciating the music. Before long you hardly perceive the music at all because you are so wrapped up in this meta-thinking about how you should be experiencing music rather than just experiencing it.

© Gary Dudney

When you are running, you have a strong sense of just being in the world.

When you're running, on the other hand, you tend to naturally get lost in the "music" that is the world around you without all the wrestling with your conscious mind. The existentialist would say that for once you simply are getting lost in being in the world, experiencing life very directly without all the filters and phobias that are usually in place. And this happens to you whenever you run no matter whether you run a long ways or just go for a short jog, whether you've just started running, or whether you've been running for years. It's pretty much a universal experience of running and available to you right there as soon as you step out the door.

No wonder that we *feel* something deeply when we run. There is a sense that we are truly engaging in life, feeling most like ourselves, feeling genuine, and feeling like we are becoming who we really are. We finish the run and feel great satisfaction, great accomplishment. We have visited a part of life that is seldom visited where we are free to be ourselves, make something of ourselves, and actualize our lives in the right here and the right now.

The great English novelist D.H. Lawrence has been interpreted as an existentialist writer, especially in his placing a supreme importance on feeling and emotion over mind and rationality when he goes to explain the essential nature of human beings. Consider this quote from his last novel, *Apocalypse* (1930):

■ What man most passionately wants is his living wholeness and his living unison, not his own isolate salvation of his "soul." Man wants his physical fulfillment first and foremost, since now, once and once only, he is in the flesh and potent. For man, the vast marvel is to be alive. For man, as for flower and beast and bird, the supreme triumph is to be most vividly, most perfectly alive. Whatever the unborn and the dead may know, they cannot know the beauty, the marvel of being alive in the flesh. The dead may look after the afterwards. But the magnificent here and now of life in the flesh is ours, and ours alone, and ours only for a time. We ought to dance with rapture that we should be alive and in the flesh, and part of the living, incarnate cosmos.

"The marvel of being alive in the flesh"—that is precisely what running allows you to experience. Running interrupts your mundane day with a chance to "dance with rapture."

CHAPTER 12

BECOMING THE MUSIC

I definitely had Georgia on my mind, but not in a good way. The rugged final 10 miles of the Georgia Jewel 100 Mile Run were taking me apart piece by piece and didn't seem to be providing any instructions for reassembly.

Just three weeks before, I had run a slugfest in Minnesota, the venerable and horrendous (for me) Superior Fall 100 Mile Trail Race, where I had been reduced to roadkill before eventually creeping across the finish line in a record slow time. Now just three weeks later, I was lined up at the start in Georgia, fully convinced that I needed a couple of additional weeks of recovery before I should even be contemplating running another hundred. But I had my reasons for being in Minnesota and more good reasons for being in Georgia, so I'd ignored the obvious fact that the races were too close together and signed up for both.

The first mile of the Georgia Jewel course travels up an asphalt road in a significant climb onto a ridge where it joins the Pinhoti Trail. My mostly local fellow runners were in high spirits, whooping it up and joking about the ordeal to come, super pumped about the challenge, while I sullenly limped along, registering one sore, unrecovered muscle group after another until pretty much my entire musculoskeletal system had checked in with my brain to report that running for the next 30 hours was not going to be possible.

I looked up at the Chatty Cathy runners steadily pulling away from me up the slope, and my one thought was, *Okay, today I'm going to find out just how tough I really am.*

I had managed to find a shuffling pace that had kept me upright and moving forward throughout the day, but sometime in the early evening, my GI tract got tired of the whole affair and took a hike. From that point on, I felt nauseous. Ginger candies and drinks with ginger weren't helping and neither were the electrolyte tablets that often rescued me from stomach problems. I couldn't look at the solid food at the aid stations, and even sipping a little broth was not sitting well with me. As the night dragged on, I could stomach less and less of the energy gel that normally provides me with at least enough calories to keep me from totally bonking on long runs, and that source of sustenance was cut off as well.

© Gary Dudney

Waiting to start in the dark at the Georgia Jewel.

NO COFFEE FOR YOU

By the time I reached the last staffed aid station with 10 miles to go in the morning of the second day of running, I had been unable to replenish my energy stores for hours and hours—really, all night. But the good news was that I had finally made it to an aid station, and I was ready to try eating again and maybe getting back into the fight. In another race in a similar situation, I'd wolfed down three slices of pizza, drained a can of Coke, and took off like I'd ingested rocket fuel, so I knew there was always hope. There was also the prospect that this aid station would have some freshly brewed, blessed coffee. I was weaving on the trail from exhaustion and taking a caffeine tablet hadn't done a thing for me. Coffee would make everything better.

So this is what I envisioned approaching the aid station. I would sit down in a comfortable camp chair and just take my time. There would be some good solid food to eat, and my nausea would have passed, so I could at last take in some desperately needed calories. There would be a piping hot plastic cup placed at my feet full of gourmet coffee because the manager of a nearby Starbuck's happened to be an ultrarunner and decided to supply the runners with comped lattes. I would sip the coffee and sort of luxuriate like I was home on my patio and eating a nice breakfast and then be on my way to tackle that last 10 miles fully restored. Life would be good again. God would be in his heaven, and all would be right with the world.

I trudged into the aid station, took off my hydration pack, dropped it in the dirt, and collapsed into a camp chair. I happened to notice a black SUV covered with dust just pulling out of the parking area next to the aid station. A hand shot out of the driver's side window waving goodbye.

"So what can I get you?" the lone volunteer at the aid station asked. It was just him and me. All the other runners were so spread out on the course that I hadn't seen anybody else for hours and hours.

"I would love it," I said, "if you had some coffee."

The guy laughed. "You know what? That's funny. We had two burners going all night, but the other guy helping here had to leave, and he took one of the burners with him. We even talked about whether we should keep the soup going or the coffee, and we decided that runners are going to need the soup more, so that's what I've got. The guy that just left took all the coffee."

My head dropped. "Okay, I'll try the soup. Maybe half a cup." But even as I spoke, I could hear my stomach warning me, *Watch it, Buddy!*

He handed me the soup. It was the same prepackaged stuff I'd been gagging on all night. On a strong stomach, it would have been fine, flavorful chicken broth with some noodles at the bottom. I'd consumed tons of it during other races with good results. But today, with my delicate stomach, just the sight of it was almost enough to make me retch. I set it down and tended to my drop bag. I got my hydration pack ready for the next and last segment of the race. It was five miles to a final unmanned aid station and then five to the finish.

"Better take lots of water," the volunteer said. "I've heard there isn't anything left at the unmanned station. They may get it resupplied before you get there, though."

This was a concern. Early on, the morning had been slightly cool, but now it was heating up quickly thanks to clear skies and a fully blazing Southern sun. At the rate I was going, it was likely to take me hours to get to the finish, as much as five hours, so even with a full hydration pack, I might well go through all my water if the other aid station didn't have any. Plus, taking a full load of water was burdensome at this point. I didn't relish having to haul around the extra weight, but I had no choice.

I tried relaxing, but it was no use. I had too many aches and pains going on. I might have tried a 10-minute nap—I was certainly sleepy enough—but I couldn't get comfortable in the chair. There was no coffee to sip, and I couldn't look at the soup. I was done with my drop bag, so the voice in my foggy head told me I might as well get up and get on with it.

I buckled the now monstrously heavy hydration pack on, thanked the volunteer, and limped off with a stale wedge of peanut butter and jelly sandwich which I had to immediately ditch. A tentative bite had me fighting off a wave of nausea before I could swallow, so that was no good. Ditto with the energy gel that I tried next. The last 10 miles were going to be done with zero energy.

© Gary Dudney

The seemingly endless Pinhoti Trail snakes through the forest in Georgia.

My slow pace made the flat sections of trail seem to go on forever and ever. Occasionally, the trail would plunge down a steep, rocky trough with tricky, dangerous footing into a forested hollow. The air was still, and it was getting hotter and hotter, and the humidity was high, so I constantly had this sensation of a clammy, dirty film covering my skin. I worked at being patient, realizing that, at this point in the race, time was going to seem to be passing extremely slowly, but I couldn't help but search ahead down every stretch of trail through the forest for a sign of the table holding the water jugs at the unmanned aid station. And, of course, my eyes were playing tricks on me and seeing tables and water jugs everywhere.

Finally, I just resigned myself to the abject misery I was feeling. The aid station would never come. I was stuck in this hot forest forever. All hope died within me, but there was nothing to do but continue. An hour later, I saw a wide space free of trees at the bottom of the valley where a couple of trails converged. It was a campground, and there sat a table with a water jug sitting on the edge and several empty containers scattered around below the table. Whether someone had gotten there with fresh water or the reports had simply been wrong, I didn't know or care. Here, at last, was the halfway to the finish milestone, and now the next stop would be the end. I took off my hydration pack, judged I could use a little more water than I had, and added some from the plastic spigot of the jug.

Then I turned toward home. The course was an out and back, so I'd be going over ground that I'd passed over before, but that had been more than a day ago, and all this part of the course we'd done in pre-dawn darkness. What I remembered was that after the initial climb from the start, we'd passed over a ridge, and then it seemed to me that we must have dropped down into a forest.

I remembered passing through trees for what seemed like miles and being frustrated by a very strange forest floor. There were rocks jutting up everywhere, sometimes long ridges of rock, and the trail took a million little zigs and zags. The running was extremely difficult. There was no way to get into a rhythm, and the trip hazard was always there. In fact, a few people had gone down around me. I couldn't see a blessed thing. I'd misjudged how long we would need our start flashlights, so I'd chosen a lightweight thingy with almost spent batteries that put out very little light and began dying on me while it was still dark. I wound up having to shadow other runners and piggyback off their lights, so being otherwise occupied trying not to trip and end my life on a jagged spire of rock, I never really got a very good sense of the terrain.

Anyway, from the unmanned aid station, it looked to me like there was a lot of climbing to do to get out of the low spot in the forest where the station was located, and then I assumed I would drop down into the weird forest where I would have to work through a few miles of bad footing and then finally get to the last downhill asphalt road to the finish.

Off I went, up an incline then through a stretch of level forest, then up, level, up. The heat was getting more oppressive with each additional hour. The mugginess had gotten worse. My skin crawled with its discomforting, gritty film. I could feel the heat radiating from the sunburn I'd gotten from the long exposure to the sun the day before. I should have reapplied sunblock back at the aid station where my drop bag was, but I'd been too blasted to think straight, so I'd blown that one. Sleepy didn't begin to describe how tired I was. I could barely keep my eyes open, and the exhaustion washed over me like waves from the ocean, constantly pushing in farther ashore over and over. My whole body felt weak from the lack of energy, but there was no way I was going to ingest any of the energy gel I had with me. Just the thought of it made me queasy.

Now I was climbing almost steadily with stretches of steep climb up a twisted path between jutting rocks. I looked up and saw a wooded ridge rising up before me that went so far into the distance that it disappeared on the horizon. *Here's the deal,* I said to myself, *get up this ridge, and then I'll drop down into that rocky forest. It's a long way through the forest, but at the end of that stretch will be the stupid road down to the finish.*

I put my head down and climbed, willing my knees to keep bending and straightening to lift my weight up the incline. This went on forever. Every time I glanced up, I would think that surely I had come far enough now that I'd get to the top of the ridge and start down into the forest, and my heart sank as I thought about how far through the woods I would still have to go. There would be no beginning of the end of this journey until I got over this torturous ridge and made the forest.

I was so far up the ridge now I felt like I was appreciably closer to the sun. The trees had thinned out, so almost all cover was gone. The sun was beating down like a hammer on the back of my neck. My feet were in agony. There were sharp pains where I'd formed and broken blisters and then just general pain everywhere else. I'd come to a place where it was almost all bare rock, the path twisting up over an uneven rocky staircase. I had to use my hands to push up through the unforgiving hard surfaces of the stone. With the effort, I could feel a fresh burst of sweat pop out on my forehead like I'd just stepped into a sauna.

AT ROPE'S END

I pushed myself up past two big rocks, the gates to hell I imagined, and lifted my head up. I thought maybe this might be the summit of the ridge, but rising before me was more trail, more incline, more rocks. I straightened up out of my crouch and suddenly felt my whole body waver from head to toe. I had almost passed out by just standing up straight. I felt dizzy and lightheaded. I took two steps and leaned over a bush and began dry heaving. It was like my body, totally starved of energy and craving sleep, was pulling out all the stops to get my attention.

The dry heaving stopped, and I took another couple of steps before I began throwing up in earnest, but there was nothing to come up except some liquid. My whole body convulsed with involuntary spasms. It felt like a demonic force gripping me and shaking me. I was bent over, hands on knees, trembling, trying to weather the storm.

It finally stopped. I straightened up and wiped the back of my hand across my mouth. I stood in the trail and fumbled for the drinking tube that was alligator-clipped to the edge of my vest. I took a long pull, swished the warm water around in my mouth, and spit it out. I took another pull, but this time when I spit the water out, from the very depths of the despair I was feeling, it seemed like spitting the water out was an act of defiance. I had hit absolute rock bottom here physically, yet I felt this strong impulse to keep going. My body seemed done, but my willpower was totally intact.

Unexpectedly, an immense and profound joy washed over me. I suddenly had a very pure and direct sense of being alive, a sense that I was totally immersed in the here and now, and the sense that I was being exactly who I was meant to be at that moment in time. For one, I was completely in touch with my body—its possibilities and limitations, its aches and pains, its requirements. Never had I felt so alive in my own skin. For another, my emotions were so visceral and tangible—the great despair I felt, but also the great determination to keep going on. My passion for running was being fully realized. And at the same time, I was hyper aware of the world around me—the pines and oaks and elms and dogwood trees, the flies buzzing by, the heat in the air, and the fins of lichen covered rock protruding from the red soil of the ridge. I felt like I was connected to everything around me, like I was seeing it all under a microscope, hearing it all through high-definition speakers. And miserable as I was, I was filled with these things and completely and utterly lost in what I was doing.

BE THE MUSIC

Recall from the last chapter the problem of really hearing the music at a concert because of the distraction of your own consciousness. Well, here, I was devoid of consciousness, or at least self-consciousness. I wasn't just lost in the music; I had become the music. My body was all the instruments in the orchestra, and the great musicians were playing directly on me. I was the trembling and weeping strings of the violins. I was the column of air vibrating inside the clarinets, the oboes, and the flutes. I was the felt-tipped hammers, thumping the steel strings in the massive grand piano. I was the drumhead, the ringing, vibrating cymbals crashing at the crescendo of the music. And there were no stray thoughts of self-consciousness, no meta-voice in my head telling me what to do or feel. I was pure music, pure running down the trail, pure being there, pure passion.

Any running experience has the potential to put you in touch with yourself, to help you transcend the workaday world, and to give you a taste of the pure joy of just being alive, but on this day, I had pursued my love of running down that rocky dusty trail so thoroughly and so beyond reason that the thrill of being alive was overwhelming. I wouldn't have traded that moment for anything despite the awful condition I was in. Friedrich Nietzsche, one of the key existentialist thinkers, rejected the notion that reason is some pure and higher form of thinking while emotions were lower animalistic reactions to the world. Strong emotions and passions, he believed, carried their own form of reason, their own insights into the world, their own way of understanding and dealing with the world. He believed passion embodies the energy that is central to pursuing one's life. Of course, passions can be base and negative, such as resentment or jealousy, but great and positive passions such as love, love of what you are doing, or love of how you are living your life, according to Nietzsche, are what make living worthwhile.

After standing there for a while, I started walking down the trail again. I felt much better. I was still just as exhausted, just as sunburnt, and just as bereft of energy, but having felt that wave of joy and having felt so thoroughly alive, the problems were now just sensations, part of the process I was going through. They were still unpleasant but inconsequential compared to how charged up I felt. Not far beyond where I had stopped, the land opened up somewhat and flattened out. There were grassy areas, now, between the trees. I was expecting to drop down at any minute into my long anticipated rocky forest when I saw a guy with a little dog walking toward me. He asked if I'd seen a tall runner with dark hair. "I've been all alone since the last aid station," I said. He thanked me and went on.

I marveled about the fact that the guy was hiking the course backward to find his runner and had come all that way through the rocky forest with that small dog in tow. He must have been walking for hours I surmised. Then, not but half a minute later, I trotted out onto a wide grassy jeep road that bent down around a curve and ran smack into a black asphalt road.

I was stunned. It had to be the road down to the finish. There had been no other road like it anywhere else on the course. What in the world had become of my miles of rocky forest?

I thought about it for a minute and then burst out laughing with relief. There never had been a rocky forest. In the dark the day before, it was the whole trip down the ridge toward the unmanned aid station that I had mistaken for being in a forest. All I had been aware of in the dark was that we kept passing by trees and the footing was terrible because of all the rocks. I couldn't see that we were up on a ridge. So in doing the long punishing climb up the ridge, I'd already taken care of my "rocky forest" without ever knowing it. I had just a mile to go now, all downhill, and all imbued with the magical restorative properties of being within a mile of the end of the race. My feet suddenly hurt less; I felt a rush of adrenaline; and now there was a little zip in my stride. I owned that last mile.

So what am I saying here, that you should run yourself into the ground until you throw up and then you will find enlightenment? No, I'm saying that running provides you with an opportunity. It is a part of your life that, if you choose, you can pursue with passion, with a passionate commitment. Georg Wilhelm Friedrich Hegel, a forerunner of Nietzsche, wrote in his *Lectures on the Philosophy of History*, "Nothing great in the world has ever been accomplished without passion." Existentialism elevates passion to a primary role in a person's quest to fully live life. Running is an area in which we can pursue a passion. And through running with passion, or doing anything with passion, according to the existentialists, comes self-awareness and self-actualization.

Heidegger makes the point that our primordial experience in the world is not *knowing* about things but *doing* things. If you build a birdhouse, for example, it is not that you know about the hammer, the boards, the nails; you use those things to engage in the task of building the birdhouse, and engaging in the task is the real, fundamental experience of living in the world, not your abstract knowledge of the nails. Running is engaging in a task, so it is a fundamental experience in living. Running gives us a chance, as Heidegger says, to take hold of ourselves, and, for the time we are running, to be authentic. Perhaps that explains the feeling of satisfaction one has after a run or the often-expressed feeling after someone has finished a 100-mile run that they lived a whole lifetime out there. While we are running, unlike during much of the rest of the time we spend in our lives, we feel in touch with our authentic selves.

The existentialists believed that the highest ideal for human beings was to accept life as your living in the world and to passionately manifest your talents and virtues. We spend a lot of our time caught in the daily rat race of just getting by in our lives. Running gives us a chance to step out of the rat race, to be fully present in the moment, to appreciate being alive, and to passionately pursue being who we really are.

CHAPTER 13

RUNNING FRIENDSHIPS

My grandfather ran the hardware store in a small Kansas town during the 1930s, 40s, and 50s—some rather consequential decades in the last century. Times were often hard, and the farmers would have to buy their supplies and equipment on credit. One of my grandfather's duties was to drive out to the fields, climb up onto a farmer's tractor, and remind him of his overdue payments.

Once, one of the older farmers passed away, and my grandfather was serving as a pallbearer. When he leaned over to lower the casket into the ground, a pen slipped out of his pocket protector and fell into the grave.

After the ceremony, a couple of the other pallbearers were grinning, and one said, "Looks like you lost your pen, Clarence."

My grandfather replied, "Oh, that's okay. He owed me money. He can write me a check."

All the time I was growing up, my grandfather had a little framed quotation on the wall above his desk. It was actually a 1925 Buzza Motto art deco lithograph. The quote was from J. P. McEvoy, who was a writer and the cartoonist behind the *Dixie Dugan* comic strip which ran in newspapers all the way from 1929 to 1966. McEvoy was the originator of the phrase, "cut to the chase," and he, rather than Mark Twain who is often given the credit, is behind the quip, "Whenever the impulse to exercise comes over me, I lie down until it passes away." Clearly McEvoy loved a good quip, just like my grandfather.

So of all the possible things in the universe that my grandfather could have had hanging over his desk, what he had was McEvoy's sentiment, "A friend is not a feller who is taken in by sham, a friend is one who knows our faults, and doesn't give a dam!"

REMOVING THE BARRIERS

I bring it up because it very much reminds me of the special nature of the friendships among runners. Developing close friendships just seems to be a natural consequence of running together. You already share a passion for running before you even begin, and then you start building a grand edifice of shared experiences together. You suffer through the heat together. You labor together over difficult sections of technical trails while going single file, and then you run miles of jeep road double track side by side. You get lost together, you race together, you do intervals together, and you finish workouts together that you thought would never end. Everything between you becomes shorthand. "Trails today or Frog Pond?" "See you on the out and back." "Jack's Peak today, but skip the loop."

Since you're both in the running mindset—that is, physically and mentally removed from your daily worries and stresses and less hunkered down in your workplace personas and masks—you're more open to each other's feelings and perspectives. The talk is less guarded and more free-flowing. Plus, you're away from all the distractions that normally make it hard to communicate with each other. There are no TV programs, no cellphones going off, and no screaming kids.

With all those barriers removed, it's just natural to get real with one another. You start talking about your problems, and the words and the deep emotions just pour out of you. Your partner tells you about his or her problems, and out there in the woods with an open mind, your empathy is strikingly apparent, deep, and authentic. You play off of each other, and before long, you're discussing your most heartfelt hopes and dreams. It's not surprising that running partners tend to "get" each other and even finish each other's sentences. To the extent that therapy is helpful by just giving you a chance to talk through your problems to a sympathetic listener, letting it all out to your running partner seems nearly as beneficial. Runners become each other's therapists, confidants, best friends, and coaches. In fact, I don't know how many times I've heard a runner talk about some enormously personal issue and then say, "You know, I've never told anybody else about that in my entire life."

© Gary Dudney

Tackling miles of tough climbs together will cement a friendship.

So now we're back to the quote. Runners don't posture for one another or manage to keep things superficial. You really get to know each other, including each other's faults and foibles. But there is something magnanimous about running friendships. You get the bigger picture of your running partner. You forgive the shortcomings. You don't "give a damn" about the shortcomings because you appreciate the complexity of this human being you are running with, and you sense how we are all struggling through this life and that nobody is achieving perfection.

Here is yet another world for you to be thinking about and exploring while you are out running. Maybe you are not becoming an expert at being mindful, or nudging yourself closer to Nirvana, or having an existential epiphany about the nature of being, but you are very likely forming some amazing friendships, and you might want to stop and think about just what that can mean. It's an opportunity for you to get outside your own little self-conscious silo of thinking and to step into other worlds.

As you interact with your friends out there so profoundly, you will get new perspectives on life. Our own perceptions of the world are always filtered through our own prejudices, biases, and selfish concerns. From your friends, you'll hear about things and ideas that are not distorted through the prism of your own worldview. As you learn to empathize more fully with another's situation, your own sense of self will seem to fade a little into the background as you become more aware of the other person's self. A Buddhist would say you are moving toward an understanding of there not being any real separation between you and others, or for that matter, between you and everything else in the world.

PRACTICAL ADVANTAGES OF RUNNING TOGETHER

Just as a practical matter, having a training partner is a huge advantage. For all the wonderful things that come from running, it still seems tough to make that decision every time it comes time to run to actually get dressed and get out the door. Once you're running, things tend to be fine, but there is always that inertia to overcome to get off your butt and start. In fact, for me, the best approach to my running routine I've found is to use this concept: Don't think about it. Rather than kicking the idea of running around and, therefore, giving the idea of *not* running some daylight, I simply throw up a mental blockade. Don't think about it. When you have a training partner, the whole idea of maybe not running gets short circuited. You've got to go run. Your partner is counting on you. Especially when you're up against a long, tough training run early in the morning, knowing that someone else is committed to doing it as well is crucial. You can't back out.

Incidentally, I apply my "Don't think about it" strategy to a lot of areas of running. Accelerate into the next interval on the track—Don't think about it. Get out of a chair at an aid station and get back on the trail—Don't think about it. Get out of bed for a long run—Don't think about it. Wade straight through a waist-deep stream—Don't think about it. It saves time and a whole lot of mental aggravation to simply launch into whatever you have to do and get it done rather than think it over and make a bad decision.

© Gary Dudney

Time and distance go by almost unnoticed when you're running with friends.

Having a partner is an important safety issue, especially if you do any of your runs in remote areas. Do you really want to be all alone five miles from your car in an area that gets no foot traffic with a rattlesnake attached to your butt? Or would you rather be out there with a friend? Two of you double the eyes and ears you bring to checking the trail for danger, and the noise you make together is going to offer bad actors in the forest more warning of your presence. You're also a lot less likely to get lost when you're running on unfamiliar trails if there are two of you trying to find the way.

Just across the highway from my home is a county park with miles of trail that gives me a perfect training venue. I was out on a run back there once rather late in the day, so I was heading up into the park just before dusk. When I looked up to the top of the jeep road I was climbing, I saw a low-slung character with a very large tail maybe 30 yards away. I instantly knew I wasn't looking at a bobcat, which I see all the time back there. This was a young, very curious it seemed from the way it was looking at me, cougar. We stared at each other as I raised my hands above my head to look bigger and slowly backed away. With a flick of its tail, it took a spectacular leap off the road and disappeared into the forest. As quickly as I could, I went back down the road where I had come from and headed straight for home with a bad case of goosebumps covering my arms. Since then, any run I take at dawn or dusk in more remote areas around my home is done with a partner.

Of course, tackling long runs with a friend is ideal. As I've noted, you're safer, less likely to get lost, and more motivated to get out there in the first place, but beyond all that, you can't beat the way the time and miles can go by almost unnoticed when you're chatting it up about all things relevant to your life. Running itself is often the topic of conversation with my running partner. We work out our training plans, decide which races to sign up for, and talk over hydration systems, shoe choices, and eating choices. We go over how the last race went and conduct a postmortem of how we did. By the end of the run, we'll have all the next steps in our training planned for the next month.

Racing with someone you've trained with is also very helpful. When race day arrives, being with your training partner cuts the stress and nervousness that big events can engender. If you're prone to going out too fast, running the first few miles at a relaxed pace with your partner can help get you off to a more realistic start. Later in the race, seeing your training partner on an out-and-back section or coming together late in the race will feel special. It can even put you in a whole new frame of mind if you're struggling.

In terms of having friends out there on race day, I should note that the trail running and ultrarunning communities are amazingly congenial and supportive. Racers in an ultra cheer each other on and are very quick to offer help if anyone appears to be in trouble. In the middle and back of the pack, especially, you would get the notion that runners are not so much competing with each other but rather trying to make sure that everyone who can makes it to the finish. Runners strike up conversations and establish friendships during ultra races all the time. As a result, people get to know each other, and a very supportive and extensive community develops in one area after another. Tap into that community, and you'll never be at a loss for company when you go out to run or race.

ROBERT'S RUN

Let's return to the theme of expanding your own horizons by fully appreciating someone else's reality and entering into their world. One of the peak experiences I've ever had as a runner was a night I spent pacing Robert Josephs, my partner during my failed Grand Slam attempt, at a later running of the 100-mile Western States Endurance Run.

Running was not going smoothly for Robert. A neurological problem was beginning to manifest itself, so his control and dexterity were suffering. The rougher the trail, the more trouble he had negotiating all the obstacles, and he would regularly catch his foot on a rock and go crashing to the ground. On one training run leading up to the race, I was with him when he took a headlong fall on a downslope and ended up sliding firmly underneath a bush. He was literally stuck there. I had to drag him out from under the shrubbery, or he might still have been there 15 years later. So even though he'd finished Western States three times before much earlier in his running life, his prospects of covering the tough, rocky course this time around really looked pretty grim. Had I been in his situation, I think I would have been primed for an early exit from the race, or maybe I wouldn't have even had the courage to take it on. A lack of courage, though, was not Robert's problem.

The aid station at Michigan Bluff at mile 55 is a critical juncture for the runners. It marks the end of a very tough section of the course and a very tough climb in temperatures that typically reach over 100 degrees Fahrenheit. Runners who are doing well come jogging down the road into Michigan Bluff, smiling and waving at the crowd. Runners who are struggling come trudging into town, wilted by the heat and exhausted from climbing in and out of the two toughest canyons, Deadwood and El Dorado.

This was my first look at Robert that day, and he was definitely a trudger. He was also late, just barely maintaining a pace that would get him to the finish under the 30-hour time limit. But the crew gathered there to help Robert through his ordeal was hopeful. We all knew that Robert was famous for struggling through the night, flirting with the cutoff times at the different aid stations, and then roaring back unexpectedly in the morning to collect his finisher's buckle.

His wife led him over to where we had set up his camp chair. He sat down heavily in the chair, clutching a cup of soup he'd gotten at the aid table. We changed his shoes and socks for him. I wiped him down with a damp towel. His wife got a sandwich into his hand and switched the soup out for a cup of ice water. He had little to say. Mostly he just bent forward with his head down.

We kept up a nice positive chatter as we worked. "The tough parts over," I told him. "Just focus on getting to Foresthill. It will be a lot cooler when it's dark. Keep drinking. Just get into the night. Finish the sandwich. You'll be okay." He listened and nodded. No one said anything about his slow pace. We'd decided to worry about that once he'd gotten to Foresthill, seven miles down the trail.

After going very still for a while, he pushed himself out of the chair and strapped his belt on. We walked in a big group down to the end of the street. Everyone was talking excitedly, full of advice. We shouted and hooted after him as he walked off down the road toward Volcano Canyon. "Way to go! Doin' great! See you soon!"

It was a full two hours before we heard his name announced at Foresthill. We'd hoped he'd make something of a comeback as the temperature dropped and dusk came on, but he had actually lost 10 minutes to the cutoff time. Again we steered him into his chair, but this time there was a rush to get him revved up and back on his feet. Unless he came alive and started making up some time, he would risk missing a cutoff on his way to the Rucky Chucky river crossing at mile 75.

After a couple of minutes of tender loving care, we were dragging him back on his feet. I had my flashlight and water bottles ready to go and was champing at the bit to get on our way. As we left, the crew shouted after us, "Run! Run!"

We trotted down the main street of Foresthill with people cheering us along as we passed the parked cars jammed up near the aid station. Farther along, the street was quiet, peaceful, and empty. The only evidence of a race going on was the orange cones spaced out before us to mark the route. We came to the final cone with an arrow pointing us down a side street, and soon we were out of Foresthill and back on the single track.

First up were several switchbacks leading downward away from Foresthill. Robert made an effort to run this section, but the trail was badly rutted in spots, and lots of loose rock made the footing treacherous. He seemed to need smooth trail to be able to run. After a mile or so, we settled into a fast-paced walk that he was comfortable with. I figured we were not going to lose any ground if we stayed with a strong walk, so I didn't push him to run. I concentrated on monitoring his drinking and kept up a little conversation to keep him occupied.

After what seemed a long time, we pulled into the first aid station, Dardanelles. I checked my watch against the list of cutoff times I was carrying. We'd maintained the same margin to the cutoff time that he'd had at Foresthill. I counted that as a success. A volunteer took charge of Robert, and I turned toward the aid table to find something to munch on. When I turned back around, I was shocked to find the volunteer helping Robert down into a chair. I had wanted to get us through this station quickly and get on our way. I made sure Robert had everything he needed and told him he had two minutes before we had to go. He munched away at a cookie, content to let me set the rules.

We left on our way to the next aid station, Peachstone, with words of encouragement drifting out to us from the volunteers. Immediately the night swallowed us up. We seemed to be next to a canyon now on our left. Above were bright stars and a half moon just over the opposite horizon. We moved along steadily for a while, but now Robert was coming to a dead stop when he took out his bottle to drink. Our pace over this section had dropped considerably from what we had managed on the way to Dardanelles. Also, there seemed to be no question about running. It was all walking. I took out the chart to see what kind of margin we had to the next station.

When the path leveled out or tended slightly downhill, I went into a little shuffle to try to spark some running, but to no avail. "We're going to have to hammer this a little bit," I said.

"I AM hammering," Robert replied, maintaining his slow walk. "This IS hammering." I had to laugh.

But the showstopper turned out to be the hills. This section of trail had a good surface, soft dirt, and not a lot of rocks, but bit by bit, we were climbing up along a ridge, and each uphill portion seemed to be exacting a terrible toll. Robert's pace dropped to almost nothing as he leaned into each climb. He could barely lift his feet high enough to clear rocks. He stumbled often.

As I checked my watch, time seemed to be evaporating. I began to calculate how much time we had to the next cutoff, how far I thought we had gone, and what pace we would need to get there. Meanwhile, Robert had started weaving from side to side in the trail. I peered nervously out to the left to see what kind of fall he might take should he actually veer off the path.

A heavy silence descended upon us as we moved slowly along. I glanced up at the stars and the moon. The night was very still, the quiet only broken by an occasional rustle in the brush. It seemed hard to believe that we were part of a major race. Nothing around us suggested any hurry. I wished that I could tell Robert to relax, that there was no rush, but I knew that our situation was getting more desperate by the minute. Meanwhile, he had become so exhausted he could barely put his bottle back in his pack after taking a drink.

"We have to be getting close to the next aid station," I said. I was guessing based on how much time had elapsed since the last aid station. But my guess turned out to be way off. We crept on, following what seemed an endless trail.

Finally, with no fanfare, no outward sign, the cutoff time for Peachstone came and went. I didn't say anything to Robert. I held out some hope that because the course had been modified for this year's race, maybe I somehow had the wrong time on my sheet. The trail at last seemed to have crested and took a sharp turn down and to the right. At the same time, we could just make out the lights of the aid station across a dark gulf in front of us. As we turned back down the trail, we actually had to walk away from the station until we finally crossed a stream at the end of a canyon and the trail twisted back around.

IT'S OVER

When we arrived at Peachstone, the aid station captain met us on the edge of the clearing. Looking beyond him, I could see people busily clearing off the aid table. I also saw a row of runners, about 10 of them, all slumped in camp chairs, each covered with a blanket. The aid station captain shook Robert's hand and congratulated him on reaching Peachstone. In his other hand, he held a pair of surgeon's scissors. "The bad news," he said, "is I need to take your wristband. You're beyond the cutoff time." And with that he carefully snipped the band off Robert's wrist. The band disappeared into his pocket. That was it.

I later asked Robert how he felt at that moment, the moment he knew he was finished. Was he angry, frustrated, heartbroken, decimated? "I was relieved," he told me.

I found an empty chair and led Robert over to it. He undid his belt and let it fall to the ground. Then he lowered himself carefully into the chair. A volunteer brought over a blanket, which I draped over his shoulders. "You did a great job," I told him. "You never gave up." He nodded and closed his eyes. "What can I get you?" I asked.

"Just water would be okay," he said. When I came back with the water, Robert had his eyes closed. I set the cup down next to his feet and looked at my watch. It was three o'clock in the morning.

All the runners sitting there were totally wiped out, motionless under their blankets. The volunteers were busy getting the place picked up and packed away. I noticed another group of people standing on the edge of the aid station clearing, talking and laughing. I realized they were the other pacers, who like me, were now stranded in the woods in the middle of the night. One pacer seemed to be in a pretty heated exchange with the aid station captain. I could just overhear him saying, "How could you not be ready to get us out of here? Didn't you know there'd be runners dropping here?" The aid station captain shrugged. He assured the guy they were making arrangements.

In fact, it wasn't long before word got around of a plan. The aid station sat at the lower end of an access road that led straight up the ridge for a mile to an another road that in turn led to the highway. The runners were to be hauled up in a trailer that had been used to bring the aid station supplies in originally. The pacers were going to have to hike out under their own power up the road.

The trailer, hitched to a jeep, was backed down into place. We rousted the runners out of their chairs and led them staggering over to the trailer. They had all stiffened up from sitting down. One runner had to be helped off a cot and complained of feeling sick. The trailer was a very low affair, the bed sitting only about a foot and a half off the ground, but even so, the runners could just barely manage getting into it. Then, once in, they had trouble bending their limbs enough to sit down. They let out rending groans as they collapsed down on the steel bed. Robert took all this very stoically, trying to do as much for himself as he could. Actually, there was a tremendous dignity about these runners as they endured this torture. They didn't complain. They arranged their painful limbs as best they could and then waited patiently for the next step in the process.

The trailer lurched forward up the road. I fell in with the other pacers to make our ascent. Despite the late hour, the pacers seemed to be bursting with energy. Finally freed of creeping forward, endlessly encouraging their flagging runners, the pacers shot up the road like the devil was chasing them. I could barely keep up. Everyone was talking and laughing, hugely relieved that at last they could move along at a good clip. What a contrast we made to the groaning cargo of runners jolting up the road ahead of us in their steel-bottomed trailer.

We reached the top and came to a big clearing in the pine trees. We unloaded everyone in a painful reverse process of what had gone on below, the runners wincing as they stepped off the trailer into our supporting arms. One runner got out and promptly threw up. I found a place for Robert on the fender of the trailer, and he sat quietly, waiting.

Soon a big suburban showed up and swung around next to us. We loaded as many people as we could, but some had to be left behind. Robert volunteered to stay and wait for the next ride. The last runner into the suburban could not negotiate the tight fit into the back seat and had to exchange places with the guy sitting in the front seat. At last settled, they were gone into the night.

Next a minivan came down the road, and the last of us were loaded in. We headed off to Auburn and the finish line at the Placer High School stadium. Once there, I led Robert down the stadium steps to the infield where the medical tents were set up. He collapsed onto a cot. I covered him with a blanket, and he immediately closed his eyes and lay perfectly still.

Winner at Western States in 2015, Rob Krar experiences hoopla and media attention. It's a different experience for those who don't finish.

FINISH LINE

My job now pretty much done, I found a place to sit down near the finish line and settled in to watch other runners finish. The timing couldn't have been better. It was just past four in the morning, so all the people arriving were earning silver belt buckles for finishing in less than 24 hours. Finishers arriving between 24 and 30 hours are given bronze buckles.

Most of the runners I saw were finishing strong, smiling, laughing, and enjoying their great success. They bounced up onto the scales for their final weigh-ins and then only reluctantly sat down to have their blood pressure checked. They were the kings and queens of the event, conquerors of the Western States course.

I couldn't help but think of the beleaguered line of defeated runners I had come upon at Peachstone only a couple of hours earlier. They had been slumped so heavily in their camp chairs, under their thick blankets, with only their sweat-soaked caps and dirt-caked legs and shoes visible. For them, time had run out. Their quest had ended miles and miles from Auburn in the dark woods with the half moon and the stars hanging over them.

But then I recalled how, as I followed Robert over the last few miles that we traveled, I had noticed that his shoulders were not sagging, his determination never having deserted him. Even as the quest became hopeless, he had continued to struggle to keep his dream alive. He never quit. He never gave up. He never lost heart. He had stayed with the race to the very end, and then with great dignity and equanimity, he had accepted that it was over. In that, it seemed to me, he had triumphed just as greatly—maybe more greatly—than the runners who I was watching cross the finish line now.

CHAPTER 14

NOT FINDING YOUR NOT SELF

When I took my first steps off the starting line of the Bighorn Trail 100 Mile Run at the bottom of the Tongue River Canyon heading into Wyoming's Bighorn Mountains, I expected a lot of things to happen to me over the next 30 hours, but having a mystical experience was not one of them.

In fact, "mystical" would have been the last thing I expected from the reality-hardened world of this rugged corner of the Old West. Sheridan, Wyoming, the nearest large town and host of the race, struck me as a completely down-to-earth, thoroughly western, hard scrabble, rodeo, non-mystical kind of place. People in Sheridan, I imagined, knew when they were only knee high to a grasshopper that you fed your stock before you fed yourself, and you didn't take any wooden nickels. Downtown was dominated by a huge tack store that had to have the largest selection of spurs ever assembled. Horses and cowboys seemed to be the theme of every bar, café, and shop in sight.

People on horseback out on the trails looked like they'd ridden straight out of a *Bonanza* episode. Hoss and Little Joe would have blended right in. At the race briefing, runners were warned to be wary going by a place called Bear Camp because there were actual bear hunters there. During the race, as I crept by the camp, feeling sort of silly in my garish running shorts, I caught the eye of a guy dressed in camo who I took to be one of the bear hunters. "Don't shoot," I joked, and he grinned.

As for the race itself, it was more of the same — earthy, not ethereal. The mud in the middle section of the race was so black, so pervasive, so penetrating, and so thoroughly disgusting that when the race was over, I took off my shoes and socks and threw them directly in the trash.

Where there was no mud, there was gnarly, rugged, slanted, rock-jumbled, single-track trail that spent a lot of time either climbing up into some serious altitude or plunging back down out of the sky. During the final stages of the race, I should also note, my feet hurt with a lot of very real and not at all mystical or mysterious pain.

Incredible hospitality and great aid stations at the Bighorn Trail 100.

But to offset all the hardships of the race, there was also some very real Western hospitality that flowed like manna from the people who organized the race. The aid stations were numerous, well supplied with soup, pizza, quesadillas, and more, and fully staffed with very helpful medical personnel wearing red vests so you could immediately identify who was going to work on your blisters. Thanks to someone doing a great job of marking the course, I followed the entire length of the trail without a single misstep. Temporary handrails had even been constructed at all the remote little stream crossings where runners might encounter slippery logs. At night, there were huge bonfires going at every aid station, even at two very remote stations where everything had been brought in by horseback. And I couldn't help but notice that lots of the work was being done by little kids helping out their elders. I've never been to a race that had more of a family feel to it.

All this is to say that the race was certainly a vibrant, vivid, and visceral experience for me and the other runners. The Bighorn Mountains were gorgeous. There were lush grasslands, alpine meadows full of wildflowers, curtains of glacially carved rock walls, pine forests, rushing rivers, and blue lakes. I expected a day and night of running through the wilderness, enjoying the scenery, struggling with the rigors of negotiating the tough trail, and finally dragging myself back to the finish just beyond the Tongue River Canyon in the tiny town of Dalton.

© Gary Dudney

Temporary handrails had been constructed to keep runners safe on slippery logs.

GOING OFF SCRIPT

But running has a way of taking the mind on adventures that are not necessarily part of the script, so at a certain point during the run, I found my mind engaged in some surprising adlibbing. It was late at night, and I'd left the muddy section of the course behind, miles 40 to 60. Back in the mud, it had taken all my concentration to navigate the trail and keep my shoes on my feet, but now I was on a long stretch of jeep road down in a canyon next to the Little Bighorn River. At 7,000 feet, it seemed like I should have been above most of the drainage, but the river here was massive. The water surged over giant boulders that pushed the blue-green water into muscular crashing cascades. In places, the road dipped right down to the river's edge. The energy coming off the water seemed palpable.

The moon cast a ghostly light over the whole scene. It was quiet except for the slap and churn of the water next to me. The runners were all spread out at this point in the race, so I was all alone in the night, and I'd gotten into a remarkably comfortable rhythm with the running. There was a slight, but steady, downhill tilt to the road, so there was no need to concentrate on my pace or stride. The movement forward was effortless, hypnotic, flowing. Whatever random things I might have been thinking about had made their appearance and then drifted away, leaving my mind essentially blank and unengaged except for the awareness of the water rushing by my side, the moonlit wall of rock next to me, the pines across the river, and the dark sky above.

Then, very stealthily, a sensation crept up on me, completely unbidden, that I was sort of disappearing into the scene around me, almost dissolving, not physically but in terms of my awareness, my conscious mind. The water surging by me now almost felt like it was flowing through me, or rather I felt like I was surging along with it, like there was a lack of separation between myself and the river. It was the same with some lanky pine trees that I could see up ahead. The river must have been up from recent rains because the trunks of many of the trees along the shore were right in the water, and the trees up ahead were partially toppled over, and their crowns were dipping into the water. I felt strangely close to these trees as I saw their branches drag and jerk in the strong current. Again, I felt like there was no barrier between myself and the trees in their desperate struggle with the river, like I was down in the water being pulled by the current, too.

I was also suffused with a sense that what I was experiencing must somehow be significant, that I had stumbled onto some truth about the world, although what that truth might be escaped me completely at the time. This reverie lasted for a short time and then vanished as soon as I turned a corner and saw the lights of an aid station up ahead. Instantly, my mind snapped back to the practicalities of what I needed to do at the aid station, how much I needed to eat, the decision to change my socks or not, whether I needed my heavier jacket, or whether my lightweight shell would get me through until morning. The odd feelings I'd had back up the road I attributed to just some random strangeness and essentially forgot about them for the rest of the race. But those strong sensations of disappearing so completely into the world had made an impression on me, and when I thought about it later, it continued to feel like I had, indeed, stumbled onto something significant.

ROBERT WRIGHT EXPLAINS IT ALL

An explanation for my mystery along the Little Bighorn seemed to come sometime later when I was listening to Robert Wright's online lecture series, "Buddhism and Modern Psychology." In fact, I found much in these lectures that tied into running and the notion that running can create some very interesting states of mind.

Wright is a visiting professor at Princeton University, an award winning journalist, author of several thought-provoking books, including the bestseller, *The Evolution of God,* and quite a profound thinker. He also is a crack-up, featuring his two dogs Frazier and Milo in some of his lectures where they are said to be demonstrating different phases of Buddhist thought or showing that a marker pen can in fact have the essence of a chew toy from a dog's perspective. His video chats on a range of issues with all sorts of intellectual luminaries on his website are entertaining and witty.

As he explains in the introduction to his lecture series, the course does not address the supernatural aspects of Buddhism, but rather what he calls secular Buddhism, or the naturalistic elements of Buddhism. He references research from modern psychology and then uses that research to evaluate Buddhist ideas. The result is that Wright can then point to some very compelling ways that Buddhist concepts, which of course are quite ancient, seem to line up with some very contemporary thinking in modern psychology.

One example, for instance, is examining the notion of the self. A classic Buddhist teaching is that the perception of a self is an illusion, and such illusions, which are built into our minds, are what lead to suffering. Wright points out that interpretations of what the Buddha actually was saying about the self vary, and an absolute rejection of something we might recognize as the self might not be what was meant, but a strong tradition has grown up within Buddhism of *anatman,* which is Sanskrit for "not self," or "no self." In this tradition, recognizing the concept of "not self" better aligns one with the true nature of the world, and a consequence is that one ceases to feel a separation between oneself and other entities in the world.

Wright explains how this Buddhist teaching might be seen as resonating with a prominent theory in modern psychology. The theory is the modular model of the mind, which, taking a page from evolutionary psychology, holds that different modules for different tasks have developed in the brain bit by bit through the process of evolution. Evolutionary psychologist, Douglas Kendrick, for example, posits a module responsible for self-protection and another module for mate attraction in a scheme that includes seven distinct modules. Modules, according to the theory, are not localized areas of the brain, but rather pull from different areas. Modules interact and cross communicate and are complex in keeping with the complex nature of thought and human consciousness. But the bottom line for the modules from an evolutionary standpoint is simply to ensure that one's genes make it into the next generation.

SO WHO'S RUNNING THE SHOW?

Modules, Kendrick explains, are active according to what is present in the environment. Two simple examples would be if a potential mate is present, then the mate attraction module would be directing behavior. If someone comes at you with a big stick, your self-protection module will come to the fore. But as noted, the modules interact and call on submodules in a very complex dance, and the switch from module to module is done without any conscious decision about shifting from one to the other. The kicker to the whole concept, though, is that apparently there is no "control" module, no one module charged with overseeing the whole process and making decisions about what happens next, which would correspond neatly to what we perceive of as the "self." Instead, there is something more like a free-for-all among modules, each attempting to follow its own agenda for ensuring survival and getting those precious genes moved along.

Of course, the modular model of the mind is supported by a good deal of research, but rather than worry about how viable the theory is or how widely accepted it is, let's just accept for a moment, as sort of a thought experiment, that it is an accurate model of the mind and then think about what that would mean. Let's also assume for the argument that who we are as human beings and what we are doing here in the universe is largely explained by the theory of evolution and the process of natural selection. That's a lot to swallow, granted, but again, for the sake of argument, let's go with it.

A cliché fits in here quite neatly: The implications of the module model *blow your mind*. Over the millions of years of our minds evolving to make us better survivors in a world of hunting and gathering, campfire etiquette and working out who gets the best spot in the cave and who calls the shots on the next mammoth hunt, each chunk of our brains evolved for a reason, to perform a particular task. We in the modern world have inherited this mish-mash of modules just like we've inherited bodies that are particularly well adapted to walking upright, running long distances, manipulating objects, and requiring a lot of nurturing before we can fend for ourselves.

So as noted before, by running, we are making a connection to this long biological past of our species and perhaps exploring or getting a feel for the nature of our true beings. Similarly, when we recognize how mental modules stand behind our thinking and our actions, we draw closer to our true nature—at least, our true evolved, naturally selected nature. And maybe a consequence of getting in touch with our modular minds is a recognition that there is no "command" module and that if you really pick apart your notions of "you" or "self," you can peel back layers like an onion until there is essentially nothing there at the center. That's quite a revelation.

RUNNING YOUR WAY TO NOT SELF

What part does running play in recognizing the nature of your mind and the possibility that no essential "self" lies at the core of your being? As I've noted before, when we venture out for a run, we break out of our standard workaday operating mode and our usual frames of reference. Sitting at your desk at work, you are deeply enmeshed in all the standard workplace concerns and activities. You are planning one project, scheduling another, meeting with colleagues to get updates on a third project, looking over the spending on a fourth. You're making notes for a presentation to your supervisor; urgent emails are demanding attention. Your phone rings, and your spouse wants some input on a social engagement. It goes on and on. The modules in your mind are on speed dial. As they deal with each task, each relationship, the modules kick in and out rapidly with you having no awareness of the process. At home with your family, there is a similar rich environment of input. Your mate retention module is in full operating capacity as you interact with your spouse. When your kids walk in the door, the module controlling raising the next generation takes hold. There are a million household tasks to attend to, supper to get on the table, neighbors to placate, and bills to pay garnering your attention.

From either work or home, when you step out that door and go for a run, you may just be venturing out for some physical activity and getting a little exercise, but ironically, your run is a mental game changer. Now all the stimuli that fire up all your modules are distant and are only in your environment if you call them up in your mind. The immediate input to your mind coming from the external world are the sights, the sounds, the smells of the forest you're running through, the street you're running down, or the field you're crossing. You may be conscious of your motion, the strike of your foot on the path, the swing of your arms, the increased exertion going up a hill, or the slight pain in your hip.

Whatever the circumstances of the run or how you feel, this is a much different environment for the mind than when you were at work or at home.

Your mental state while running is similar to meditation in that you've narrowed down the immediate focus of your attention and quieted much of your mind's activity. The modern psychologists would say that you've limited the activity of most of the modules or turned them off altogether. In this atmosphere, the stray thoughts bubbling up into your conscious mind are now very recognizable. They seem to stand out in high relief. You're running along, and suddenly you're thinking, *Maybe I should call up Bob and apologize for being so negative this morning?*, or you start planning dinner, or you remember a scene from the movie you saw last week that made you cry. You can think of each of these thoughts as a module trying to get your conscious attention, trying to get its work done, moving its agenda forward.

As these thoughts arise—these attempts by your modules to coopt your attention—it's pretty easy in the context of your running experience—since they seem sort of out of place like intruders at a wedding party—to regard them objectively, turn them over in your mind, and then dismiss them. We harken back to the mindfulness technique, and as with mindfulness, you limit your attachment to the thoughts and avoid identifying yourself with them. They are thoughts thrown up from different modules; they don't constitute "you." So running becomes a stage on which you rehearse this notion that you are not your thoughts, that within your mind there is a collection of interconnected, active modules that take turns dictating your actions. You get a feel for the process as you objectively observe thoughts bubbling up and tugging at your attention.

BACK TO THE LITTLE BIGHORN

In his lecture series, Wright references the American philosopher William James' definition of mystical experience as including two key features. One feature is that the experience has been *noetic*—that is, one feels as if some profound knowledge or some deep insight has been imparted. The other feature of a mystical experience, per James, is that the experience is *ineffable*—that is, one finds it very hard to express just exactly what the knowledge or insight is. The new understanding one has attained defies description. Actually, that is kind of convenient, isn't it? You have a mystical experience, but then you turn around and say, "Wow, I just learned something really profound, but hey, I can't exactly tell you what it is or describe it to you. You just have to take my word that it was super great!"

So to an extent, I have to take that dodge. In that moment that I was running along the Little Bighorn River and went from being sort of lost in the rhythm of running to feeling like I suddenly had disappeared and then felt a very strong connection to all the things around me, it did feel like a deep insight into the nature of things, or maybe the nature of me. It is also hard to describe exactly what that feeling was or put into words how that connection felt and how it was different from just normal being fully aware of things as one is when one is being mindful. But this felt more profound than that, and here would be my guess as to what had happened.

© Rob Mann

Discovering my "not self" in the woods at night?

I think for just a brief period I was free of the illusion of "self." I wasn't identifying myself with any of the activity of my various mental modules, and at the same time, I wasn't suffering from the notion that somehow there was a controlling module that was in charge. I had slipped into a very deep state of awareness of what was around me, but I wasn't misidentifying that sense of awareness I had as being "self," or being "me." It was just awareness. With the lack of a sense of self, I also had a feeling that now there was no barrier between myself and other things. If you are not a self-contained little unit of "self," then there is no self to be separated from other things. The result is a feeling of connection, or a feeling of the interconnectedness of things. You have a more fluid interaction with things outside of you. Between you and the world, the boundaries are less rigid. Thus, when I felt the presence of the river, I felt very connected to it, like I could feel the flow going right through me. I saw the water tugging on the branches of the pine trees dipping down into the river, and it was like I felt the tug myself.

The whole experience was fleeting, vague, insubstantial, and confusing, but I believe that there, on the banks of the Little Bighorn in the ghostly moonlight, I was getting just a glimpse into the Buddhist notion of *anatman*, of "not self." Of course, it didn't persist, and I am only taking a stab at what I thought happened there, but for now, as a couple of well-known ultrarunners who will recognize this quote always say, "That's my story, and I'm sticking to it."

Runners often find themselves with an inability to explain just exactly what they find so appealing about running. Sometimes, especially after a very hard or challenging effort, they even feel transformed, reborn, and reanimated by the experience. They feel their experience was transcendent. Perhaps, if it were suggested to them, they would be happy with the terms noetic and ineffable. Perhaps, out on the trail, completely lost in the experience of running, they caught a glimpse of not self as well. That's my story, and I'm sticking to it.

CHAPTER 15

FOUNTAIN OF HEALTH AND YOUTH

It's tradition at the runners' orientation meeting the day before the 100-mile Western States Endurance Run to recognize notable runners in the field—the defending champions, male and female, and others who have gained entry by winning races around the country or by placing near the top in the previous year's Western States. The men who are being recognized tend toward serious demeanors. Most of them make a minimal show of acknowledging the applause when they're introduced. They keep it all business, serious competitors facing serious competition.

The women seem much more relaxed. They smile and step forward when it's their turn, waving genially, pleased as punch about being there and getting recognized. One woman, however, stands out. She's slim, cut, and lean like the other women. She moves just like them. She smiles and waves just like them. She's just a lot older. Her name is Gunhild Swanson. She actually didn't make it through the lottery for the 2015 race to get one of the coveted starting spots, but she'd received a notice from race management that she'd be entered under special circumstances, a category reserved for a handful of runners who have some unusual claim at getting a chance at the race. Swanson's circumstance was that at the age of 70, were she to finish, she would be the oldest woman ever to have completed the tough 100-mile trail race under the 30-hour cutoff.

The race begins at five o'clock in the morning with a brutal climb from the Squaw Valley Ski Resort to the top of Emigrant Pass, a vertical rise of 2,550 feet over four and a half miles of dirt road and trail. Having lucked out with the lottery for once (in the past I'd been picked once in nine tries at a time when the chances of getting picked were about 50/50), I was there and pushing myself fairly hard up the mountain, determined to get off to a good start.

Near the top of the climb, scrambling up a steep pitch on a rocky single track, I noticed the person climbing next to me was none other than Gunhild Swanson. She was having no more difficulty with the climb than I was. She seemed calm and happy. Once we'd reached a more level, wider road, I asked her if she had any secrets for retaining such a high level of fitness through her sixties. She said there was no secret; she just liked to put in about 55 or 60 miles a week, running trails near her home in Spokane, Washington. We went over Emigrant Pass, and in the rush down the other side of the ridge, I lost track of her.

Much later in the race, I'd gotten across the river at Rucky Chucky, mile 78, and had just started the two-mile hike up to Green Gate when a woman with a very young pacer went by me. It was Swanson again with her 15-year-old grandson, who looked thrilled to be up in the middle of the night. He was out in the woods taking grandma for a big hike. I congratulated her on how well it was going. At that point, we were on pace to finish with about an hour to spare, a nice comfortable margin, and she looked as spry and energetic as she had way back at the start. With my own fish to fry, though, I again lost track of her and couldn't have told you if I wound up ahead of her or behind her at that point.

I pushed hard to cover the final 20 miles of the race, eventually making it to the track at Placer High School in Auburn to finish in 29 hours and 17 minutes. The almost 45-minute cushion I had to get under the cutoff had made the final miles very relaxed and carefree for me. After walking around a bit on the infield of the track, I pulled a plastic chair into some shade, sat down, and savored my finish and the knowledge that I no longer had to get back up and start running again.

THE FINAL FINISHER

With less than 20 minutes left in the race before the 30-hour cutoff was imposed, John Medinger, the announcer at the finish line, came on the loudspeakers and said that Swanson had made it through Robie Point, which is the last checkpoint 1.3 miles from the finish. I'd forgotten all about her. It occurred to me that she must have struggled over the last 20 miles since I had gotten so far ahead of her after Green Gate.

The author driving toward the finish at Western States.

Twenty-two-year-old Katie Trent, the youngest female finisher and 48 years younger than Swanson, appeared in the stadium and finished with about five minutes to spare. There is always a lot of drama at Western States about the last finisher. Will someone claim the belt buckle with just seconds left on the clock? Will someone make it to the track but then not get to the finish line before timing out?

With just a couple of minutes left to go, John Corey came through the opening in the fence where the runners first step onto the track. The crowd in the stadium began cheering for him. He was going to finish about half way through the final minute of the race. It looked like he would be the last successful finisher and that Swanson wasn't going to make it.

Then, through the normal jumble of noise and voices that arises from the infield of the track where all the finishers and their crews are celebrating the moment, cheers and applause and screams could be heard from the street just outside the stadium. Gunhild Swanson burst onto the track surrounded by a knot of runners trying to help her along. Rob Krar, the winner of the race some 15 hours earlier, was there, running in sandals and giving her advice. Tim Twietmeyer, five-time past winner of the race, was with her and several friends and relatives. Swanson elbowed someone aside to get to the inside of the track. She had 90 seconds left to cover the 300 meters that lay between her and the finish line.

As she ran, she was like a magnet pulling the people from the infield out toward the track. Medinger started calling down the seconds remaining. Everyone began shouting encouragement. She made the last turn. Her entourage peeled away save for her pacer who ran along next to her down the final stretch. People were yelling for her to RUN! RUN!

She crossed the finish line and entered the record books with only six seconds to spare, the final finisher and belt buckle winner of the 2015

Western States Endurance Run in a time of 29:59:54. You could hear people saying, "Oh my God! Holy shit!" Medinger called it the most exciting moment he had ever witnessed at the finish line of Western States in 33 years of watching the drama unfold there.

Having personally shared a little bit of the adventure with her and having just experienced the same hot, brutal 100-mile course, I was as thrilled and as appreciative as anyone with her accomplishment. But I couldn't get that incredibly tight six-second margin out of my mind. A little pause along the way, an extra bite to eat at an aid station, a little less energy to push over the final mile, and she would have faced colossal disappointment rather than triumph.

When I'd seen her at Green Gate, she had looked plenty strong. Yet I'd managed to open up an almost 45-minute lead on her over the last 20 miles. I concluded that her age had just caught up to her, and while I'd been able to run hard to the finish, she had floundered out there until she'd made it to the stadium with just those few seconds to spare. *It must be tough to be old*, I thought.

I couldn't have been more wrong. In fact, what had happened is that at mile 88 she had followed a couple of other runners off course. They'd done a long climb that wasn't part of the race, and by the time they'd backtracked to the correct route, they had run an extra three miles. (Going off course is fairly common in ultras. As long as you return to the point you departed the course on foot and without assistance, there is no penalty.) Swanson would have had about the same comfortable margin that I had at the finish, but, instead, she had to face the anxiety of losing all her hard-won margin-of-error time and then had to run a stellar final 10 miles to get under the wire. So much for my theory that her age had caught up with her! She had run almost exactly the same race that I had.

ULTRA AGING

In the same issue of *Ultrarunning* magazine that previewed the story of Swanson's attempt at the record at Western States, there was an article about 80-year-old Bill Dodson who had just broken the American age group record (80-89) for the 100K by over two hours. A week later, he broke the American 50-mile age group record by over three hours. Yet another article in the same issue featured 60-year-old Mark Richtman who had also been demolishing records for his age group (60-69). At the Lake Sonoma 50-Mile in 2015, he notched a 7:52, making the 60-69 record at that race almost 20 minutes faster than the 50-59 age group record. Richtman set another stellar age group record at the Miwok 100K, which, like Lake Sonoma, is among the most competitive races in ultrarunning.

What in the world is the deal with these senior citizens running such fast times at such long distances? Swanson and Richtman maintain workout routines that include high weekly averages, especially Richtman, at 85 to 90 miles a week. Dodson eschews the high mileage for track workouts, strength training, and lots of racing. All three seem to contradict the notion that running is some kind of zero sum game in which you start out with joints that will deteriorate with use, so the more you run, the quicker you will inevitably wear them out.

In fact, the whole sport of ultrarunning offers evidence to refute that notion. Younger runners are gravitating toward ultrarunning nowadays, somewhat changing the demographics of the sport, but, traditionally, older runners made up quite a significant portion of the participants. And this in a sport where the shortest race distance is five miles beyond what would be the finish line for a marathon. Today, runners over the age of 50 constitute about 20 percent of the entrants of most ultra races. In the past, that percentage was even higher. For example, at the 2013 running of the Arkansas Traveler 100, of the 77 runners who went the whole distance and earned their belt buckles, an amazing half of them were 45 years old or older. Two 49-year-olds even finished in the top five. Running, it seems, is well suited to older individuals, and ultrarunning allows them to show just how far the envelope can be pushed.

AGE SLOWS RUNNING, BUT RUNNING SLOWS AGING

It has been well established that regular exercise is a key to maintaining health as you grow older. Running is an excellent choice for meeting this exercise requirement as it is a relatively low-impact activity and easily adapted in terms of intensity and quantity. It has a wide-ranging impact on the cardiovascular system, muscles, joints, and connective tissue. And, as we've established, the mental benefits of running can be substantial. As long as you need to exercise to stay fit, why not choose running? Moreover, the notion that running causes joints to deteriorate is not born out by studies which find no more incidence of osteoarthritis in runners than in non-runners. And though some would argue that moderation is essential, in fact, ultrarunners show no more propensity toward injuries, such as stress fractures, than other runners.

In an article in the *New York Times*, Dr. William Roberts, a professor of family medicine at the University of Minnesota Medical School and the medical director for the Twin Cities Marathon, is quoted as saying, "Aging is a use-it-or-lose-it proposition. Continued exercise throughout a lifetime will reduce the rate of loss of strength and endurance, likely improve quality of life and help maintain balance, which reduces falls." Use it or lose it. Apply that concept to running in particular, and you are talking about using or losing heart health, endurance, balance, stamina, respiration, circulation, joint health, and muscle strength, especially in the lower body. These are all things that would be high on anyone's list for what they would most want to preserve as they grow older.

© Gary Dudney

John Mark is having no trouble crushing a sub-24 finish time at the Javelina Jundred in the Arizona desert at age 52.

PLAY IT SMART

In fact, many people discover running only after they've hit their forties or fifties. Brand new older runners need to start small and work up. They should mix jogging and walking into their workouts and stay comfortable. Weekly mileage should be increased slowly, no more than about 10 percent at a time. They should also consult a knowledgeable shoe expert to get a quality running shoe that is the right type and fit.

Those who have been running for years might want to make some adjustments to their routines as they get older. It's a good idea to mix some strength training (free weights, calisthenics, Nautilus) into the routine. With age comes a natural loss in muscle tone and strength that can be counteracted. Runners will tend to lose upper-body strength as they get older because those muscles aren't being worked as much. Some upper-body weight training will help preserve proper running mechanics. Older runners should also stretch more to maintain muscle flexibility.

Another good strategy is to switch out one or two runs a week for a cross-training activity such as swimming or biking. What wear and tear does occur on joints and connective tissue will be reduced with these low-impact activities and will help avoid the runner experiencing burnout and overuse injuries.

Older runners tend to gravitate toward longer, slower races and ultrarunning events. This makes a lot of sense because the LSD (Long Slow Distance) workouts that target long races are much better suited to older runners than the stressful tempo runs and risky interval workouts that target fast 10K times. It also makes sense to spend more time running trails and less time on roads or other hard surfaces. Trail running is more forgiving on less resilient muscles and joints, and the uneven surfaces will keep the muscles that stabilize the stride well conditioned.

Older runners should cultivate a studied indifference to race times which will inevitably slow as one grows older. Now is a perfect time to stop worrying about the clock and instead focus on the whole process of running—the journey, including the scenery, the communion with friends, the satisfaction of completing a new distance, or running a new course. Running can become more about an inner journey and less about the physical components of racing and competing. Although, some runners will discover a whole new motivation for racing because of age group competitions.

Finally, everybody should make a habit of going in for a thorough checkup and battery of tests appropriate for their age group. High blood pressure, high cholesterol, and diabetes are just a few conditions that often present themselves later in life. It also is wise to work with a doctor who is knowledgeable about helping runners stay active in the sport.

© Gary Dudney

John Mark wading the San Lorenzo River near Santa Cruz, California, still going strong in an ultra 10 years later.

YOU'RE HOW OLD?

It's a common experience for avid runners to have non-running friends of the same age who just seem frailer and much less physically capable than themselves. Think of the contrast between Gunhild Swanson running strong at the end of 100 miles at Western States and most people her age, or compare Bill Dodson breaking the age group American record for the 100K to most 80-year-olds. The health-inducing benefits of running are definitely in the mix of the things that made it possible for these remarkable individuals to perform the way they did.

So here is yet another aspect of running to focus on when you're out there shredding a gnarly trail or putting in that last interval on the track: Running is keeping you young and healthy, every step of the way. It's like Dr. Spock is standing next to the trail or next to the track, flashing you the Vulcan hand gesture and solemnly wishing you to "Live long and prosper."

CHAPTER 16

ONE HUNDRED MILES

Let's talk about running 100 miles, or, more specifically, let's talk about *you* running 100 miles. You probably have some questions. For instance, you might ask, is there any reason to believe that I could ever do that? And the answer is, yes, there is every reason to believe you can do it. If you have trained for and run a marathon, for example, you are probably capable of running much farther and likely up to 100 miles.

Running shorter distances, you tend to run as hard as you can from the start and pour it on right up to the finish. No wonder at the end of a half marathon or marathon you feel totally spent. Running mega distances, like 50 or 100 miles, the strategy is totally different. Your goal is to run within yourself throughout, so the way you feel at the end of a marathon is no gauge for how you will feel at mile 26 of a 100-mile run.

Even if you've never run a marathon, if you learn to run regularly and do your share of long training runs, you can aspire eventually to running 100 miles. It is not the superhuman, impossible feat that you might think, although it does rank pretty high up there on the scale of things that are likely to impress. Normal people train for and finish the distance. Being a super athlete is not a prerequisite.

In fact, there is something of a boom going on in the 100-mile race industry. Many people are out there discovering the joys, heartaches, rewards, and whipsaw emotional roller coaster of running the big distance. In 2014, for instance, there were about 7,000 runners who finished a 100-mile race in North America, and interest in the distance is still growing. Not that long ago you could count the number of 100-mile races on your fingers and toes. There were a handful of older classics but not much interest in starting new events. That situation has changed dramatically. The number of well-supported 100-mile races has exceeded 150 events in the United States alone, and you are finding 100-mile trail races being staged all over the world. Many events have become so popular that you need to get through a lottery to even get your chance at toeing the starting line. But don't let that stop you. Nowadays, there are events available on almost every weekend of the year and spread from coast to coast where entry is simply first come first serve, and there are plenty of open spots.

WHY BOTHER?

Another question, of course, is why would you want to run 100 miles? Given the fifty thousand other reasonable things in life you might commit your time and energy to, why choose this as a goal? Because it will be one of the most amazing journeys you will ever take in your life. At a time when the term *epic* has become a toothless cliché, when every small-scale enterprise is labeled epic, when a large slice of pizza is called epic, or getting off work a half hour early is said to be epic, a 100-mile run actually *is* epic in the original and true sense of the word. It is epic in scale and in distance. It is epic in the pain and suffering it engenders. It is epic in the vast emotional range that it puts you through. It is epic in the journey that you will go through within your own mind. Guaranteed.

 Ironically, the 100-mile race is an enormous physical undertaking, yet the people who have run the distance credit their minds with being the key to their success. One oft-heard saying goes, "You run the first fifty miles with your legs, the last fifty with your mind." Another runner said, "Mental fortitude is more important than physical endurance." And yet another quipped, "90 percent of ultrarunning is 100 percent mental." At one point, I had finished my first 50-mile race and couldn't imagine running any farther. I said to my friend who had already done a 100-mile race, "I get running fifty miles but how do you run the last fifty?" He said, "Oh, the last fifty, that's all Zen."

The 100-mile distance forces you to be resourceful with your mind. It causes you to explore and discover new ways of thinking about what you are capable of and who you—when pushed to your absolute limits—essentially are. And that, in turn, explains the logic of including 100-mile running in this book about the mental aspects of running. Perhaps you could run shorter distances and keep your thinking superficial and never enter into any of the various states of mind described in this book, but just try to run 100 miles without tapping into some deeper resources in your mind, and you will very likely come up short.

WHAT DOES IT TAKE?

What does it take to run a 100-mile race? What secret formula do those finishers at the Western States Endurance Run follow to win through to the end? Basically, it comes down to three things. They have put in enough training miles and long runs to have built the strength and stamina it requires to go that far. They have learned to eat and drink properly so their bodies stay adequately hydrated and fueled. And they have developed the necessary mental fortitude or mindset to carry them through to the finish despite all the expected and unexpected problems they will have faced on the trail. Master these three requirements, and you could be there in Placer High School stadium in Auburn, California, finishing Western States as well.

The training to build the strength and stamina is pretty straightforward. You need to put in a lot of miles and a lot of time on your feet. An average of 40 to 60 miles a week is standard, sustained over five or six months with an occasional "easy" week to give your muscles a chance to rest. The key workouts, just like with marathon training, are the long runs done weekly or every two weeks, where you cover 20 or more miles, and you stay on your feet for five or more hours. Doing the long runs on hilly terrain and technical trail will amp up the difficulty and effectiveness of the training. Added endurance also comes from running back-to-back long runs on successive days, working out twice in one day, or going out for 20 miles the day after a race. Running on fatigued legs when you really want to stay on the couch is, incidentally, an excellent test of your willpower.

You can get invaluable experience and gauge where you are in your training by entering a series of ultra races—distances of 50K, 50 mile, or 100K—leading up to your 100-mile attempt. A 100-kilometer race or a difficult 50-miler will give you some sense of the strains you will feel during 100. Plan to do some of your long running at night to get used to running with lights. You'll also gain some experience with that midnight to six a.m. stretch of sleepiness that you'll have to cope with in a 100. Also, run long in the heat, in the rain, in the cold, or in other adverse conditions. You'll learn how to perform under less than ideal running conditions, make yourself more resilient, and find similar conditions during the race less formidable.

No matter how well trained your muscles become, you will not make the distance without replacing the vital fluids, electrolytes, and calories your body needs to keep functioning for so long. Depending upon the difficulty of the course, 100 miles is going to take between 24 and 36 hours to cover. You need to learn how to eat and drink so that you can stay out there and keep moving forward for that amount of time. Your fluids will come primarily from water or sports drinks. The sports drinks have the advantage of containing lots of additional electrolytes.

It used to be that runners were encouraged to drink as much water as possible, something like a 12-ounce bottle per hour, but lately there have been concerns about overdrinking and bringing on a condition called hyponatremia, which is a dangerously low concentration of sodium in the bloodstream. "Drink when you're thirsty" has become the new rule of thumb, rather than trying to stick to some drinking schedule, but, of course, you need to drink enough to offset the sweating you're doing and stave off dehydration. Continuing to have the urge to pee from time to time and producing a strong, clear stream are considered signs of good hydration.

© Gary Dudney

Learning to eat and drink will be a major part of your training. During the race, you'll get fueled up at the aid stations.

What to eat, how often to eat, and whether to eat specialized energy gels or bars versus just regular foods are topics that are endlessly debated among long-distance runners, and it seems that each runner eventually has to work out his or her own unique preferences. One way or another, you have to take in sufficient calories. The trick is to do so with a mix of foods and special energy-supplying products that will provide you the calories without upsetting your stomach, which is under a lot of stress during an ultra race. You'll want to find out what works for you by experimenting during your long training runs and pre-races with all sorts of different foods and energy products. By the time you're ready to tackle the 100-mile run, you should know what works for you and what doesn't. Trying out new things on race day can end in disaster.

Finally, there is the mental component of the race or the mindset necessary to complete the distance despite getting to the point of physical exhaustion and wanting to quit. It will take tremendous willpower and sheer determination to get you through a 100-mile run, but these are qualities that you can work on before the fact. In the latter stages of your long runs and during the shorter ultras you do to prepare for the 100-mile race, you'll face moments when the fatigue and other problems will conspire to make you want to give up. That is when you need to work on using different mental techniques to keep going. Practice repeating a mantra to yourself that will replace the negative thoughts with something affirming. Work at accepting the painful feelings and seeing them as a positive, as proof that you are giving your maximum effort. Break the running down into manageable segments and congratulate yourself on each segment completed. Focus on what you need to do for yourself to keep going right at the moment rather than thinking about the whole piece that remains. There will be high points and low points during your long runs and races. Get used to the fact that the low points will occur, but also trust in the fact that things can change. As one runner put it, "It doesn't always keep getting worse."

© Gary Dudney

Be sure to train in less than ideal conditions. It will get you ready for whatever conditions you'll face during your big race.

Another thing to be aware of is that you will be facing many problems out there that you did not foresee or expect. Over 100 miles of trail, things are going to happen. You should be ready to roll with the punches because you're going to get punched. Your hamstring may go south, your knee may go south, your ankle, your toenail. Name a body part, it might go south. You may trip and fall down over one of ten thousand roots or rocks; you may even fall off a cliff. You might dump your iPod in a river, leave your water bottle at an aid station, get stung by angry wasps, follow the wrong trail to nowhere, put your foot down on a rattlesnake, do a face plant in a rock garden, get blisters on top of blisters, throw up, lose heart, get dizzy, or get to the end of your rope. The trick is to realize ahead of time that anything can happen, so when something does happen, you don't get discouraged and think, *Oh, something went wrong, I guess this is not my day*. Something is always going to go wrong—for you and everybody else—but it can still be your day.

LOGISTICS

Just as a practical matter, you should be prepared for the fact that the logistics for participating in a 100-mile race are a lot more complicated than for shorter races and require fairly extensive preparation. First you'll need to make your travel plans for yourself and possibly your crew. Most 100s can be tackled solo, but a supportive crew and pacer can be very helpful and can make the difference between success and failure. If you get a chance to volunteer at a 100 or serve as a pacer or crew member for a runner, do it. There's no better way to learn what to expect for your own attempt. Race orientations are usually held on Friday of race weekend, so you need to arrive Friday afternoon at the latest, and you should consider staying through to Monday as you may be totally wiped out on Sunday after your finish.

Use the race information received prior to the run to educate yourself and your crew on all the driving directions, aid station locations, and calendar of events. The aid station mileage chart and past race results can be used to work out a rough schedule for when you expect to arrive at different aid stations. Once you have a guess at when and where you'll be on the course, you can prepack your drop bags and crew bag with the food, supplements, night running gear, extra clothes, and other items you'll need during the run. Check the race information for weather predictions and learn what you can about the course layout. No plan will be perfect given all the unexpected issues that invariably crop up over 100 miles of trail, but good preparation will give you the best chance of having what you need when you need it out there in the cold and dark.

You can also increase your chance at success by picking an "easy" 100-mile race as your target race. Not all 100-milers are built the same. Some 100-mile courses work hard to make you fail. They offer up steep ascents when you're on your last leg; they scatter rocks everywhere so no step comes without a little extra effort; they knock you out with tight cutoffs; or, alternately, fry or freeze you to death. But then there are other courses that seem to ease you on down the road. When you need a break, they provide a long gentle downhill. Their trails are smooth as glass. They feed you well, bring you in for a rest when you are weary, and aren't too fussy about how long you take.

Not surprisingly, mountains increase the difficulty of a course. Mountainous courses tend to feature lots of elevation change, and with every thousand feet of elevation, you lose a percentage of your running capacity. Mountain trails also tend toward the steep and rocky. Smooth trails and roads that change elevation only gradually encourage you to keep chugging along. Loop courses can be more manageable than point-to-point courses. A typical loop course often returns you to a big supportive start/finish aid station where you can rest, regroup, and get off to a fresh start. Loop courses also reduce the chance of getting lost since you're traveling familiar ground later in the race as opposed to always facing new territory, especially when night falls. A race with moderate temperatures also keeps you from having to deal with high temperatures, which increase the risk of dehydration, and freezing temperatures, which can quickly sap your resolve to continue if you're not well prepared for the cold.

RIO DEL LAGO

What is it actually like running 100 miles? Here is a blow-by-blow account of one of my 100-mile runs. There was something of a unique shitstorm in the way my stomach reacted to the race, but in a 100-mile run, there's always something. Rio was pretty much the usual parade of expected and unexpected problems.

"Could it be any hotter?" I asked myself, sitting at the Friday afternoon race orientation for the 2011 edition of the Rio Del Lago 100 Mile Endurance Run. I'd dressed for the weather in a light t-shirt and baggy shorts. I'd also found the shadiest spot on the patio of the community building at Beal's Point on the shore of Folsom Lake near Sacramento, California. But I was still sweating to beat the band.

Meanwhile, the race director of Desert Sky Adventures, Molly Sheridan, was all joy and light, talking about the next day: "Awesome aid stations...hoping for a record number of finishers...great weather... fantastic course." I looked down past an expanse of green grass at the lake shore where a swim team was doing laps around a set of orange buoys, and mothers were watching their kids splash in the water. A ferocious, glaring sun sizzled above in the sky. Tomorrow I was going to run 100 miles. Just crossing the parking lot to get to the orientation had seemed like an endurance event to me.

A bunch of scantily clad teenagers paraded by, laughing, their hair wet and dripping, teasing each other, young, carefree and cool in the heat and the sun. Watching them, I felt ancient at age 58, like an old man swept up in the Crusades, marching in the sand, clad in hot leather, outside the gates of Jerusalem on a misguided quest. Run 100 miles...in this heat...at my age...am I crazy?

Race day began at three the next morning. I armored up with sunblock, skin lubricant, bug spray, Band-Aids, and hydration pack and stepped out of my air-conditioned hotel room into what should have been a comforting morning chill. Instead, I felt a warm envelope of sticky air seal shut around me.

The race began in the dark with a little out and back on a bike path to kill a couple of awkward miles. I made my first mistake when I dumped my flashlight passing back through the start. It stayed dark for another hour, which I spent creeping out other runners by snuggling up close to them to piggyback off their lights. With the dawn, I could relax, stop stepping on everyone's heels, and enjoy the beguiling parklands next to Folsom Lake where we were running. The farther we went, the more rugged and picturesque the lakeshore became. The trail rose and fell and curved in and out through the canyons above the water. We passed Horseshoe Bar and then Rattlesnake Bar. Some thin but strategically placed clouds dampened the sun's early morning fire. I managed to get up the switchbacks of Cardiac Hill and on into Auburn Dam Overlook at mile 25, feeling pretty human. At that point, hope sprang eternal.

But leaving Auburn Dam Overlook and dropping down into the canyon toward No Hands Bridge of Western States fame, I could feel the angry heat taking hold. Soon I was reduced to a walk as I tried to keep my core temperature from rising and blowing all my valves. At just that moment, my iPod shuffled randomly onto an old Cole Porter classic, "It's Too Darn Hot." *Gee, that helps*, I thought grimly. The heat persisted as I crossed No Hands Bridge and struggled up K-2, a steep and broken road with several false summits that toyed with me like a cat might toy with a desiccated mouse.

Next came a largely exposed seven-mile loop beyond the Cool Fire Station. The irony of arriving at a town named "Cool" at the hottest point in the race was so thick you could have spread it on a bagel like cream cheese. As I trudged around the endless loop, a woman on horseback pulled up next to me. She asked how long the race was, and I told her it was 100 miles. She laughed and said, "Well, you picked the hottest day of the year to run that far."

Back at the aid station at the firehouse, I dropped into a chair. My two crew members, David Nakashima and Robert Josephs, huddled around me, looking concerned. It was midafternoon and 40 miles into the race. I should have been wolfing down sandwiches to stoke up my energy reserves for later, but my stomach was off, and the nausea made me uninterested in food. It was all I could do to choke down a little banana and a few chips. I waved off the peanut butter and jelly sandwich and the hot soup they offered, thinking that when the sun went down, my appetite would return, and I would catch back up with the eating.

I tore myself out of the chair and crept along a section of heat-radiating blacktop road to the Maidu aid station and then down to the aid station at the bottom of Cardiac Hill to reach 50 miles. Here, the course offered up a mind-numbing challenge, a back-and-forth section of all fairly rugged single track that went: Cardiac Hill to Rattlesnake Bar to Horseshoe Bar to Twin Rocks (turnaround) to Horseshoe Bar to Rattlesnake Bar to Cardiac Hill (turnaround) to Rattlesnake Bar to Horseshoe Bar to Twin Rocks, and only then to the finish. Runners tenderly referred to this part of the run as the Meat Grinder.

Luckily, far down below us, there were pleasure boats cruising up and down in the blue waters of Lake Natoma. The people on board were stretched out in the late afternoon sunshine like sleepy cats, quite oblivious to the drama playing out on the dusty trails above them. Oh, wait. That just made it worse. The full day of mega-heat had chiseled me down to a nub. I was barely negotiating the uphill sections of the course. On the flats, I was into a survivor's shuffle. On the downhills, gravity was all I had going for me. My stomach was not coming around, so I was falling way behind on replacing my energy stores. When the darkness finally closed in around me, the night air was warmish and offered no relief.

Okay, I thought, *things don't look too good, but I have some clean socks in my drop bag at Rattlesnake Bar, so I can do something about my feet.* A gritty dust had been seeping into my shoes and socks all day, combining with the heat to create, basically, sandpaper against the soles of my feet. On a positive note, the pain from the resulting blisters was keeping my mind off my sour stomach. When I got to my drop bag at Rattlesnake, there were no socks. I realized they must be in my bag at Horseshoe Bar.

By the time I got to Horseshoe Bar at mile 60, my mind was in an uproar. Everything hurt, not just my feet. My stomach was a mess. I was getting sleepy and exhausted. I hadn't eaten hardly a thing all day. I managed to get my hydration pack filled. I fumbled through my drop bag for electrolyte tablets and energy gel, and I left, forgetting about the socks. *Idiot!* I thought, as I realized what I had done about a half-mile from the aid station. I consoled myself knowing that I could get socks from my drop bag at Twin Rocks. Six miles and an eternity later, I arrived at Twin Rocks and discovered I didn't have a drop bag there. No bag, no socks, no nothing. This was discouraging.

INTO THE MEAT GRINDER

Sometime after midnight, my stomach had had enough and took charge. I heaved three times in a row before I could wobble off down the trail. I tried to make the best of it and convinced myself that I was now a lot better off. I could start over with the food, the liquids, the energy gels, and the salt tablets and maybe get to a better place. Plus, at Horseshoe Bar, my pacer was going to join me, and I could get my feet fixed up. I could still make it. I just had to keep going all night.

The curious onlookers gathered around my blistered feet at Horseshoe Bar were clearly impressed with the awesomeness of the damage to my feet. They shook their heads. They said, "Wow." They all agreed that nothing could be done. "They've already popped," the guy holding my foot explained. "I'll just clean them up, and you can put on the clean socks. Nothing else I can do." I stared dully at the top of the guy's head who was telling me I was going to run 10 more hours on painful feet. David handed me a sandwich, which I gnawed on listlessly. I was thinking about quitting. I'd counted on some kind of miracle with my feet, and that wasn't happening. David shrugged. "Just give it some time," he said when I told him I might drop.

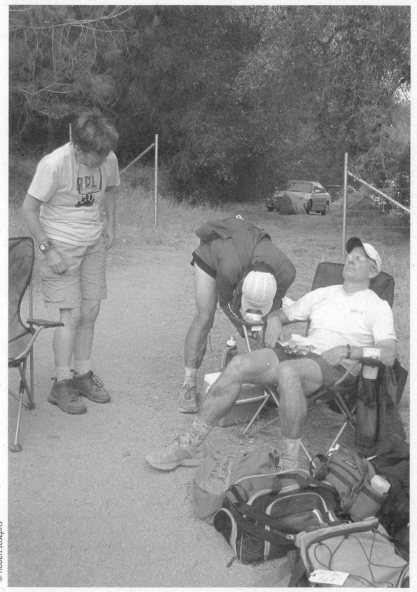

© Robert Josephs

Dead in the water at Rio del Lago surrounded by concerned crew members, but I managed to get up and keep going.

I sipped soup, ate the sandwich, and stared into a campfire. After 15 minutes, David said, "We better get moving." From pure instinct, I got to my feet and left the chair of defeat behind. We walked a few steps out of sight of the aid station, and I threw up behind some bushes. David patted me on the back until I straightened up, and we moved on.

Ever so slowly, we made our way back to Rattlesnake Bar and then on to Cardiac Hill. At each aid station, I would collapse at once into a chair and doze for 15 or 20 minutes while David waited and timed me. I kept drinking and eating, thinking that finally I would be able to keep something down, but, invariably, as soon as I was up and moving, I would start retching again. It got so ridiculously bad that it started to seem funny. I would straighten up and smile at David as if to share the joke. "How frickin' pathetic is this?" At the bottom of every uphill, I would have to stop, bend over and rest my hands on my knees while I steeled myself for the effort of climbing onto a rock or up a slope with absolutely zero energy to draw on. I was tripping on every bump in the trail, weaving into the weeds, and sweating from the effort even though I was barely moving.

Eventually, my stubbornness paid off. The morning light began to come up. David pushed me along until we got to Twin Rocks, the last aid station, and I had only five more miles to go. We worked out the time remaining before the final cutoff at the finish, and it looked good. As long as I kept moving, I would make it. Robert was going to pace me on in from there. I was still unable to eat, but somehow I found energy and strength in knowing that the last aid station was behind me and only the finish line remained. Each step remained painful, but now the last step was not so far off.

Slowly we completed the final stretch of trail and came to the dirt road that skirts Folsom Lake. The road rose and fell, and I trotted down the backside of the hills just to show myself that I could still run. Then we were on the causeway crossing over Folsom Dam, and in the distance, I could see a big red arch marking the finish line. I didn't hurry. I could have run the last half mile, but I just walked and savored the moment.

I jogged the last few steps and passed under the finish banner. I was the next to last runner to complete the course under the time limit. It had taken 31 hours and 20 minutes. More than half of the starters had succumbed to the heat and quit. For just a few moments, I was buoyed up by the tremendous thrill of being done. Finisher's belt buckle in hand, I posed for a few photos with David and Robert in front of the big race banner. The next thing I knew, I was sprawled out on a patch of grass. I could feel the earth pressing up against me, supporting my back, my arms, my legs. After struggling for so long, now at last I could just exist with no effort. David and Robert went to pick up a car that had been left at an aid station. When they returned, I was all alone. Everyone else had packed up and left. You would have never known that an event had taken place there.

Back at the hotel, I watched from my bed as Robert did all the packing, loaded up the car, and checked us out of the room. All I had to do was get up, walk out to the car, and fall into the back seat. Robert would drive us home. But there was just one more thing I had to take care of. On my way out to the car, I stopped by the bathroom to complete my Rio Del Lago adventure. I threw up.

© Gary Dudney

Sometimes the road can seem impossibly long and the end impossibly far away.

CHAPTER 17

QUITTING

Running offers myriad pathways to bring you closer to an understanding of your true self (or, for the Buddhists in the crowd, your true "not self"). Out on the trails, or even in the depths of that fifth full race-pace quarter-mile repeat on a fancy college track, your mind barrels past all the self-conscious masks and egoistic smokescreens that usually layer up your identity and gets you more in touch with your core being. This self-discovery process may need a little goosing. As we've seen, by running mindfully or concentrating on being in the moment, you can enhance the possibility of getting by the obstacles and learning more about yourself.

But there is nothing like running hard enough to get you to the point of wanting to quit to fast track opening up a window into just who you are and what you're made of. You may be oblivious to all the other possibilities for self-discovery afforded by running, but when you push yourself to the limit, it's inevitable that the mental high drama that follows is going to make you do some deep-dive soul searching.

It would be hard to comprehensively cover the mind of the runner without touching on the subject of quitting. Quitting, to be sure, is a mental process, not a physical one. Yes, your physical body may be screaming at you to stop the pain, end the torture, but *you* get to decide how to react to those signals. You can endure them, or you can give in to them. It is a conscious mental decision. Barring actual injury, the body is usually capable of going on whether you choose to go with it or not.

THE SEDUCTION OF QUITTING

By quitting, we're talking about dropping all the way out of a running effort, such as stopping halfway through a long training run or giving up decisively on a particular goal, such as backing off the pace that you're trying to hold to break your 10K PR. We're also including both racing situations and workouts. So, in fact, you're in quitting decision mode fairly often if you're an active runner training for faster times or for completing a first marathon or an ultra or just doing a lot of running in general.

Every time you take on a tempo run or jump on the track for intervals, you are going to find yourself out of your comfort zone and edging up to that threshold where you want to give up on the intensity. The long marathon training runs are always going to put you in the danger zone for quitting as you test yourself against distances you've never run before. When you finally get to your target marathon and try to hold your pace over those last six miles, you will marvel at the difficulty of it all. The same will be true for the third mile of a fast 5K or the fourth and fifth miles of a 10K PR attempt. Continuing to push hard enough to achieve your goal can seem practically impossible. The first time you try a 50K ultra (31 miles) or any ultra distance, you will venture into new territory and face fatigue and stress of a whole new order from what you're used to, and this stress will be extended over miles and miles of trail and hours on the clock. At least with a 10K you might have a mile to go to get it done. In an ultra, you might have 20 miles to go to get it done.

And here is the thing about quitting: It is instantaneously a tremendous relief, which is what makes quitting so enticing and seductive. It's like mainlining heroin. One instant you are straining to hold your pace, every part of your body is screaming for a release, your muscles are locking up so you're fighting hard against yourself, your will power is going AWOL, and you know this awful pain will only get worse and worse. Then there is a little click in your mind, and suddenly you see it isn't worth it. It makes perfect sense to quit. Nobody is going to die here. You back off just a little bit, or maybe a lot, and, instantly, in the blink of an eye, quicker than thought, Bob's your uncle, you are flooded with infinite relief. It feels so good so quickly physically that your first impulse is to wonder how you could have made it so far without succumbing. In an ultra, you might spend hours fighting off the urge to quit. When you finally relax, plop down in a chair, and say "That's it," the relief is enormous and instantaneous.

Of course, once you've quit, you now have a lot of reckoning to do with yourself. You've learned something about yourself. You've discovered the threshold of pain and suffering that would make you quit. Later on, you may question your decision—you may even beat yourself up about the decision—but it is not going to change. You don't get a Mulligan. It now is what it is. It's in the history books.

The other possibility is that you face that infinitely seductive compulsion to quit, but you don't. You keep up the suffering, you endure the abuse, you win through, and you finish at your target pace, or you cross that first marathon finish line, or you complete your first ultra. How much sweeter is the taste of that triumph having faced down that moment when you wanted to quit? It's the old Thomas Paine sentiment, "What we obtain too cheap, we esteem too lightly: it is dearness only that gives every thing its value." Facing down that heart of darkness in the middle of your attempt at a new 10K PR or in the middle of the night at some godforsaken ultra and continuing on, that is what gave your effort its special dearness and that is what you will be taking away from the experience. Again you will have discovered something about yourself, but this time you'll have discovered something very positive. You came to that point where you wanted to quit, but you didn't. You persevered.

MECHANICALS

Now, of course, the dynamics are completely different if you suffer a "mechanical" and then are forced to quit. Should your leg become detached from the rest of your body at the hip, then it's not your day. If you fall and break something, if a muscle tears badly and the pain definitely persists, if you roll an ankle and a huge bruise appears on the side of your foot and it swells up to the size of a grapefruit, if you are gaining weight noticeably and your renal system has shut down, or if you should suffer any other kind of truly threatening medical condition, the smart and correct thing to do is quit.

There is some wonderful footage of a runner at an early running of Western States, a woman who has fallen down and gashed her knee all the way to the bone. The doctor attending her is trying to pull her from the race, but she insists on going on. He finally reluctantly agrees that she can continue as long as she's gentle with the knee and only walks from that point on. The final clip of the film shows her up the trail, checking back to see if doctor is still watching her. When she sees he's turned his back, she disappears around the corner, running.

There is another clip from Western States showing a runner sitting in the darkness of a nighttime aid station. The camera lights him up garishly. He's taken a spill and broken his collarbone. It would seem that it's not his day, but that's not how he sees it. Since he figures he doesn't technically need an intact collarbone to run, he has the medical staff wrap his whole upper body with gauze so his good arm is free and the arm on the side of the broken clavicle is immobilized against his body. He runs off into the night and eventually finishes the race in Auburn.

These are examples of extreme pluck and guts but not very sound thinking. If there is a clear risk of further injury or permanently damaging something or putting yourself in a position where other people have to take risks to rescue you, then you should withdraw with a clear conscience and take comfort in the fact that quitting in such circumstances is the right thing to do. It's not like you're quitting just because you feel like something the cat dragged in. In circumstances where you are truly putting your health in danger, just remember, there will always be another race or another opportunity to run your heart out. It might even be the same race the next year, which, on the positive side, will afford you an opportunity for one of the greatest thrills in running: coming back to an event and getting it done after falling short the first time.

The author mid-race feeling like something the cat dragged in.

The same logic applies in a situation where you don't actually drop out of a race, but an injury causes you to slow down and fail to make your target speed goal. Better safe than sorry if there is a chance that you are doing yourself legitimate harm. I was once trying to qualify for the Boston Marathon. The race I was in had lots of pace runners who were there specifically to help people like me. I stuck like glue to the pacer who was going to get me just under my qualifying standard until mile 20 when I suddenly felt an evil pull in my right hamstring. I'd been looking forward to mile 20, thinking that if I was still on pace there, I'd be practically unstoppable; but the pull happened at the exact instant I went by the mile marker like it was radiating some kind of bad juju at me.

I held my pace for a while and kept my place next to the pacer, but I could tell I was making the injury worse, tearing more muscle fiber as I continued to push. I tried cutting my stride length down and speeding up my turnover, which helped relieve the pain a bit, but now the gap between me and the pacer slowly started to widen. When I sped back up to narrow the gap, the pain worsened. I realized I could probably stay with the pacer and qualify, but it would be at the risk of really damaging my leg, or I could back off, finish the marathon, and try to qualify some other time.

I sadly watched the pacer slowly parade off over the next hill, and eventually I limped in over the finish line, missing my qualifying time by a little over a minute. The injury cleared up after a couple of weeks of rest and recuperation, and I was good as new. I couldn't help but think of a running friend who had a permanent lump of scar tissue in one of his hamstrings that always checked his speed and got sore when he pushed hard. It's impossible to be sure, but I might have been saving myself from his fate even as I watched the pacer disappear ahead of me that day. I also saved the plane fare to Boston.

FORGET PLANNING AHEAD

Some running pundits advise you to imagine ahead of time what circumstances would cause you to quit, and then, presumably when you found yourself in those circumstances, you'd say to yourself, "Okay, so that's it. I'm done." I don't think this works.

First of all, there are so many things that can go wrong in a race or during a workout and no way to predict which injury or accident may occur that you almost never foresee the problem or problems you actually end up facing. Then, when something does occur—a twisted ankle, a bout of nausea, an unfamiliar pain in the knee—it is usually not immediately apparent if it is a showstopper or not. So the decision about quitting is going to involve ambiguous, unforeseeable circumstances. What are the chances that your preconceived notions about quitting will apply?

Plus, quitting is all about your mental state right at the critical moment when you are feeling at your worst. There is no way sitting in your armchair next to a cheerful fire, smoking your pipe and taking your slippers from your loyal dog's mouth, that you're going to be able to imagine the mental frame of mind that you'll be in out there on the trail. That's the thing about quitting and what I experienced the first time I ran in Leadville. Beforehand, it's easy to imagine that nothing could make you quit. You have this well of grit and determination. But when you're actually out there in the dirt, and your problems are mounting like locusts, and you've burned through all your patience and all your mental resources to stave off the discomfort, it's a different story. In the event, instead of experiencing this deep well of resolve or this bulwark of thick stone between you and giving up, your mental resources have been whittled down until you are on a hair trigger to throw in the towel. It seems like the slightest little additional problem will spill you over the edge.

The circumstances can also make quitting seem like no big deal. Why worry about failing occasionally during training runs? You go out for the 15-mile long run called for in your marathon training, a brand new distance for you, and from the start you struggle. The course is hillier than you'd thought. The sun is out, and it's too hot. You're getting a pain report out of your left calf, or you're getting shin splints again. You're out of water. At 10 miles, you're desperate for relief. Maybe you're not recovered from last week's effort? Why not just drop out of this workout and pick it up next week?

You might face a similar situation in an interval workout. You're not quite hitting the times you'd hoped for. Halfway through the drill, the intense pushing is getting unbearable, and you're falling short of the goal. Your legs feel dead today. "Screw it. I'll come back and do it right next time," you conclude. On this point, I have a couple of general running rules that I always try to follow, and one of them applies here. My rule is: Never drop out of a workout. The reason is that running into trouble during a workout is a golden opportunity.

As I said before, quitting is a mental operation, and the mental state that you find yourself in just before quitting is unique to the situation. You can't put yourself in that kind of mental distress abstractly ahead of time. So getting yourself worked up enough to want to quit during a workout, which is essentially a dry run for the real event, is a gift because now you have an opportunity to practice *not* quitting. Pay careful attention to these moments. Here is your mind not unreasonably making the case for quitting: "It's just a workout. Sheesh, what's the big deal?" And it might seem like a very strong case indeed, but by ignoring that logic and carrying on with the workout, you practice denying that inner voice its victory. The mind commands such and such. You ignore it and keep going. The more you practice facing down that quitter voice, the better you get at it.

THE CLASSIC MISTAKE

My record as I write this for finishing ultras that are less than 100 miles long—that is, 50Ks, 50-milers, and 100Ks—is 94 finishes and 1 drop. The one drop came at the 1996 running of the Quicksilver 50 Mile/50K, and, in fact, I finished the 50K, but I had signed up for the 50 Mile, intended to run 50 miles, and when I quit at 50K, I considered it a failed attempt at 50 miles. So what would have been a perfect record of finishing ultras of less than 100 miles is marred by that one drop.

At the time of that race, I was a novice ultrarunner and prone to making every mistake in the book, although my mistakes usually didn't result in DNFs. This one time, however, I was tripped up, but what I have come to think of as the classic mistake when it comes to deciding to quit is making a *hasty decision*.

It was an unusually hot day. It seemed like every race I entered that year had record high temperatures. I'd gone out hard, as was my habit back then, and gotten well behind on my hydration. I was running too fast, trying to keep up with runners who were only doing the 50K. By the time I was near the 50K mark, I was definitely dehydrated and in major distress. I was nauseous and headachy, dizzy, and lightheaded. I could feel that my core was heating up. I had stopped sweating. When I ran my hand over my forehead, it was dry and clammy. Pulling into the start/finish area where the 50K ended and the last 18 miles of the 50 miles began, I recognized I was suffering from heat exhaustion, and any more running might be dangerous.

There didn't seem to be any ifs, ands, or buts about the situation. I had ominous symptoms. The afternoon was hot and getting hotter. I couldn't imagine continuing to run and not getting worse. So I went straight to the first guy I saw with a clipboard and told him I was dropping out of the 50-mile race. "You sure?" he asked.

"Yes, it's too hot," I said, and so he marked me out of the race.

I started to head for my car when I noticed a runner fishing a can of soda out of a big ice chest that was sitting there. I was in no hurry. Since I wasn't running the last 18 miles, I could drive home leisurely and still be home much earlier than expected. I took a can of soda for myself, wandered over to some shade, and made myself comfortable with my back against the trunk of a tree. An enormous sense of relief flooded over me. I was done running, and the worry about dying from the heat was gone. I sipped my soda and absently watched runners coming into the finish area and some starting back out to complete the 50 miles.

I couldn't have sat there more than three or four minutes when I realized that I was feeling a lot better. I stretched my legs out, and they were sore but seemed just fine. I'd definitely cooled down. My core was under control, and I could feel the normal process of sweating in response to the hot air. When I stood up, all the nausea and dizziness were completely gone. *Uh-oh*, I thought to myself. I walked out to my car in the parking area. I was literally trying to get myself to feel some distress, some sign that I was still in danger of melting down in the heat, but it was no use. I really felt pretty great.

It struck me that almost without a doubt I could have finished the race. I had just needed a break to cool down, and not even that long of a break. If I'd gone back out, I would have had to have slowed down considerably, given the heat its due, and walked a lot, but I was certain that I could have gone that last 18 miles safely.

Of course, I should have found the guy with the clipboard, told him I changed my mind, gotten something to eat, and then run back out on the trail. I kick myself to this day for not doing that, but mentally I was just too far gone, too completely checked out of race mode to do that. It was just too compelling to think of it as a done deal. I'd already officially withdrawn. That was it. Go back and run in that fierce heat for four more hours? Forget it. I got in my car and drove home.

So based on this incident and many others that followed over the years, I would say the first rule to follow in a quitting scenario is don't be hasty about making your decision. No matter what the situation, give yourself some time. Drink or eat or dunk your head in a bucket of ice water. Do whatever it is that might help counteract your problem and relax. It shouldn't make any difference if you quit right this second or 15 minutes from now. So take those 15 minutes to let your body rest and your mind calm down and consider your options dispassionately. Things can change even though it doesn't seem like they will. If you still need to quit, the extra time was no harm, no foul. If you don't quit, if you rise from the dead, you might have a story that you'll be telling your grandkids.

THE KEY TO NOT QUITTING

So quitting is seductive; you can't plan ahead for it; and when things are at their worst, you're tempted to rush your decision and get it over with so you can just lay down in that blissful shady spot in the grass or get back to that hotel room where you'll feel human again instead of feeling like Robin Williams in the jungle in the movie *Jumanji*.

Moreover, in something like a 100-mile run, it's usually not just one problem that has you up against the wall, but a whole cluster of problems working together to sap your resolve. You've got blisters crying out to you from both feet; it's gotten dark, and you can't keep your eyes open you're so sleepy; your stomach has been in riot mode since early afternoon, so you're way behind on eating enough to supply the energy you need to keep going; you've slowed to a crawl; it seems to be taking forever to get to the next aid station, and when you check your watch and do some projecting of time and pace, it doesn't even look like you'll make the final cutoff at the finish anyway. Gee, you're looking pretty bad. Then you kick a half-buried rock so hard that you're certain you broke all the toes on that foot.

Now is certainly the time to shuffle through your playlist of mental strategies for dealing with painful situations. You can try associating your discomfort with the fact that it is normal to be feeling such strains when you are performing at your best and all the other runners are coping with similar discomfort. You can try repeating your mantra, replacing the negative thinking with something affirming and positive. You can treat the pain in a mindful way, sinking down into it for a moment, recognizing it as just another sensation, avoid attaching yourself to it, and then moving on to other sensations in your environment. You can experience the pain as part of the "being there" of existential existence. You can even crank up your actual playlist and try to replace the pain with a focus on the music or turn to your friend who is out there with you and try to distract yourself with some gallows humor.

But let's assume that all these strategies prove insufficient weighed against the enormity of your problems. That negative, inner voice breaks though all your defenses. *Okay, that's it,* it says to you. *Your pace is too slow to finish from here. You're not eating, so you'll have no energy, and you already feel incredibly weak. Your stomach will never feel any better. You're going to fall asleep on your feet and fall over. Your feet are torturing you, and that's going to get unbearable. Be smart and quit now. Why prolong this useless suffering?*

Here is why you should prolong the suffering. First of all, in any difficult run, you are going to experience highs and lows in your condition—peaks and valleys. You are definitely in a valley when you have sunk so low that you want to quit. When you're in a valley, it's hard to believe that anything will ever change, that you will ever feel better than you feel right then. If you just keep going, though, keep putting one foot in front of the other, things often do change. As one ultrarunner was quoted as saying, "It hurts up to a point, and then it doesn't get any worse." Against all expectations, you might get back to a peak or at least make it to a less deep, more manageable valley. The only way to give that a chance of happening is if you keep going.

But this is a logical argument and one you throw up against the logical arguments being put forward by your inner voice telling you to quit. Your mind will lay out its case and present you with a lot of overwhelming and convincing evidence for quitting. But the key to not quitting is that you have to simply ignore what your rational mind is telling you. And you can do this because you are not going to be trading much in rational stock anymore anyway.

You are going to tap into the emotional side of your mind where irrational thinking has its home. You are going to let sheer determination outweigh all that evidence being thrown at you. Now we're back to Hegel, "Nothing great in the world has ever been accomplished without passion." Determination, here, is the form your passion needs to take. You have to invoke your passion, your passionate desire to keep going. This determination will be unthinking and unreasoning; it will ignore all the voices in your head telling you to quit. As long as you burn with that determination, it will sustain you. It will allow you to keep going. If you lack determination, nothing else will get you to the finish line. If you have determination, nothing can stop you.

Run with determination and nothing will stop you.

OPPORTUNITY

The pickle you are in by the time you feel like quitting is horrifying and can feel utterly hopeless. Yet in this great adversity, there is a very hard won opportunity for you. Edgar Allan Poe said, "Never to suffer would have been never to have been blessed." Only having gotten to this point in your run, when you are forced to summon up all of your determination and tap into that irrational passion that is within you, are you able to broaden your notion of your own self and find out what is truly there. You will be blessed with a greater insight into yourself, but this wasn't going to happen without the suffering coming first. Only now can you recognize that the rational mind is only part of who you are and that you have capacities and emotional strength that you may not have known was part of you.

Thomas Paine said, "These are the times that try men's souls." Now is the time that your soul is being tried. What will you discover when the chips are down and all seems hopeless? Give yourself up to the passion. Run with determination and marvel at what you are capable of when you tap into this area of magical, irrational thinking.

© Gary Dudney

The rapture of being alive.

QUITTING

EPILOGUE

LANDING

"Keep life and lose those other things."

From Lao Tzu, *Tao Te Ching*

I hope this book has changed your perspective on running, that you've become more thoughtful about your running experiences, and that you've learned to take a Taoist approach, recognizing something of the essence of running and how it flows with the rest of your life. I hope you can't run anymore without many possibilities for how to think about running going through your head.

I hope you're more focused on the journey you're taking when you run and not so much on the end result. I hope you're staying relentlessly positive, running mindfully, and getting in touch with your inner trail monster. I hope you're chilling out, having an existential experience, finding your passion, becoming the music, making close friends, not finding your not self, and staying young. I hope you're seriously thinking about running 100 miles and not quitting.

Running, as I've said before, is a gift. To be able to put other areas of our lives aside for a while, to get out the door, to run down a trail, to allow our bodies to move as they were designed to move, to get our daily exercise—these are all good things, but there is a potential in running for much more. Joseph Campbell in his famous series of conversations with Bill Moyers, published under the title *Joseph Campbell and the Power of Myth,* says: "People say that what we're seeking is a meaning for life. I don't think that's what we're really seeking. I think that what we're seeking is an experience of being alive, so that our life experiences on the purely physical plane will have resonances within our own innermost being and reality, so that we actually feel the rapture of being alive."

Running can be a life experience that resonates with our innermost being. What is it about running? It is, I believe, that when we are running we sometimes "feel the rapture of being alive."

CREDITS

Modified cover graphic: ©Thinkstockphotos/iStock

Cover design, layout & typesetting: Sannah Inderelst

Copyediting: Elizabeth Evans

Managing Editor: Sabine Carduck